Yamashita's Trucks of Treasures

Flames of the Golden Trail

Paul Roderick A. Ysmael

Published by Kaibigan Books
Los Angeles, California, USA
March, 2014

Gen. Tomoyuki Yamashita.

Paul Roderick. A. Ysmael

Copyright

All rights reserved. Printed in the United States of America. No part of this book may be used or reproduced in any manner whatsoever without written permission except in the case of brief quotations embodied in critical articles and reviews.

ISBN-13: 978-1497455115

ISBN-10: 1497455111

Paul Roderick. A. Ysmael

Publisher
Kaibigan Books

Disclaimer

Stories and views expressed by the author are his own and do not necessarily reflect the editorial position of this publication or of the publisher or printer. Kaibigan Books does not knowingly publish false information or infringe on the authors' copyright and may not be held liable for such and for the views of the author exercising their right to free expression.

Paul Roderick. A. Ysmael

Acknowledgments

To the Holy One up there, for giving me hands and a pen.

To my Papa Julieto and Lolo Ilong, for the fatherly affection and paternal inspiration.

To the people of Cervantes, Ilocos Sur, for their heroic deeds during the war.

To our neighbors and relatives in Salugan, especially those who still patronize our sari-sari store, for sharing this story.

To Mang Bernie and Atty. Ming Masangya for their efforts, time and sincere support in helping me secure the copyright of this book.

To all those who, in one way or another, shared in the writing, reading and sharing this book, truly you are part of the treasures of the world.

To all those who believed, for giving me a chance to be a storyteller; especially,
HJI.Mhd.Perfecto Manzano Pascua
and Percival Campoamor Cruz

Maraming salamat po!

Photo credits: Google Images for downloaded photos. Original owners of photos could not be ascertained.

Paul Roderick. A. Ysmael

Dedication

For my wife Cris, the treasure of my life.

Paul Roderick. A. Ysmael

Foreword

Legend has it that hoards of treasures, which are part of the Japanese Imperial Army's loot from various temples and museums of Asia that date back to the Old World were stocked by the Japanese in Fort Santiago, Manila during the last year of World War II or in 1945. The treasures came from Old Babylon, the temples of India and Southeast Asia. Fearing confiscation by the British forces that were controlling China if they transport it by land, the precious loot was shipped by the Japanese from Singapore to the Philippines by commandeering civilian merchant vessels. Sometime in July 1944, after crossing the Sulu Sea and the West Philippine Sea the said ships unloaded treasures at the Port of Manila. When the Japanese forces were already certain of their defeat in the Philippines, they chose to retreat towards the mountain ranges of the Gran Cordillera taking with them their looted treasure. They used the rugged and seldom used trail going to Bessang Pass at Cervantes, Ilocos Sur and planned to cross the mountains and escape through the Pacific Ocean using the natural port of Palanan at the eastern tip of the Province of Isabela.

The Japanese did not know that a group of fierce and determined guerilla forces numbering less than two hundred knew their plan of escape. This guerilla force was after the trucks of treasures that they are planning to bring to Japan. Amidst the fighting to either end or prolong the war, these two groups of brave soldiers were on their own "specialized"

Paul Roderick. A. Ysmael

missions. One group was tasked to protect and the other is tasked to recover the same trucks of treasures. Both groups were ready and able to kill and willing to be killed, in the name of their sacred missions either in the name of their Emperor on the side of the Japanese or for the Filipinos, for their love of their newly liberated nation.

Set in the panoramic mountains of the Gran Cordillera and nestled inside the small, sleepy valley town of Cervantes, this story of the flaming path where the looted treasure traversed remains a legend to the rural folks until today. This is a narration as to how a peaceful town became an unwilling host of war that ravaged the virginity of its placid forests fertile land and where the incessant wailings of its women sounded off the destruction of its soul. Heavy fighting, torching of homes, tortures against the innocents and killings at its most violent proportion drenched the pristine rivers of the town with blood. The war likewise scattered tons of mutilated corpses of soldiers and civilians at its fertile land. Its mighty mountains were stunned to shame that it just opted to hide behind the fog instead of protecting the town from all those years of battling. The fog was forced to cover the mountains to in order to prevent the latter from witnessing the destruction that they cannot endure.

This is a story of the men who risked and, some even lost, their lives in securing the said treasures and the men who likewise offered their lives in pursuit of the same. This is "Yamashita's Trucks of Treasures:

Paul Roderick. A. Ysmael

Flames of the Golden Trail," the first of the trilogy on the missing trucks of treasures of World War II.

Paul Roderick. A. Ysmael

About the Author

Atty. Paul R. A. Ysmael obtained his Bachelor of Laws and BA Political Science, cum laude, degrees from the University of the Philippines where he also served as Chairperson of the premiere state university's student council. He used to write for the UP Sinag, a campus features magazine and became its Managing Editor.

He hails from Cervantes, Ilocos Sur, married to Mrs. Cristina Ledesma-Ysmael and lives in Antipolo City.

The author is presently Vice President at the BPI Legal Affairs Division, formerly the head of the legal department of Philippine Savings Bank and former president of Centennial Savings Bank.

Paul Roderick. A. Ysmael

Introduction

Our "sari-sari store" (the local name for a convenience store) is located at the western tip of the poblacion (town center) of Cervantes, Ilocos Sur in a district called Sitio Salugan in Barangay Rosario. Sitio Salugan or "Salugan" is a community of small professionals, local politicians, farmers and farm workers. The farmers and farm workers till plant and harvest at the rice fields and sugar cane plantations in an adjacent agricultural valley called the "Tamaang

Paul Roderick. A. Ysmael

Plains," a vast and wide rich agricultural land sandwiched by the hills and mountains of the Northwestern Cordillera Mountain Range. The plains until this day is irrigated by three small creeks that come from the water falls of the tallest mountain in the area, Mt. Namandiraan that towers more than 6,500 feet.. The Tamaang Plains is one of the five major agricultural plains of the town, and perhaps the largest one. These plains are largely devoted to rice, sugar and corn. Tropical vegetables are grown on the sides or as intermediate crops, in between harvests. These plains and its surrounding mountain ranges are the reason why Cervantes is the largest Ilocos town in terms of land area.

Sitio Salugan is therefore "home" for about a hundred families of farmers and farm workers that till the Tamaang plain. A simple landmark of the community is our little store. People looking for relatives and friends in the area normally get their information from my grandparents who manned the store on a daily basis. My grandparents knew every person living in the community including their schedules, work locations, nearest relatives and even their in-laws. Sometimes in a desperate attempt to collect the debts of the store's clients, even their visiting relatives are informed how much do they owe the store and for what items which they purchased composed their debts.

The store has been there since the Spanish colonial times and had been managed by our family's older generations to serve the needs of these farmers, who are mostly our relatives. It has played the role of a

Paul Roderick. A. Ysmael

general supplier and center for social interaction among these humble farmers. Typical of any rural convenience store, we sell anything from Abaca to Zipper. We sell various types of bagoong (fish sauce), tuyo or dried fish, cooking oil, kerosene, beans, peanuts, soft drink, liquor, from canned goods, garbage cans, fertilizers and farm tools. During the rainy season where there is no harvest, we even sell the farmers' product – rice. If you are a farm worker, name your needs and we have it, except burial services. There is also a couple of bench and a table in front of our store, where our customers can have a free coffee in the morning-- if there is an available supply and more importantly if my grandfather woke up with generous mood, which is seldom among Ilocanos. Later in the day, travelers and salesmen can drop-by for a bottle of soda and in the evenings, men straight from the farm consume several bottles of the national Filipino gin-- the Ginebra San Miguel. Their "cuatro cantos" (four cornered bottles) of the Gin is perfectly matched by newspaper roasted "dilis" (fried fish) or in times of drought, salt and red pepper to refresh their tired muscles after their day-long work in their farms.

When I was in my elementary and high school years, from 1977 to 1988, I helped tend this store. It is the morning shift which I hated most. This is the store's version of "rush hour" that begins at around five o' clock or even earlier. During this hour, children and/or wives come to buy their needs for their farmer family breakfast. You will understand my childish annoyance to this hour of the day. As an example, we already sell on retail 250 milliliters of cooking oil which we repacked into used bottles of gin from a 100

Paul Roderick. A. Ysmael

liter, but still, they will buy a retail of around 1/8 of the bottle or even less. And also you have to divide the retail pack of the 12 pieces of dried fish into four as they request for retail of the retail pack. This daily practice is repeated on other merchandise that is sold in volume like vinegar, kerosene, liquid fertilizer and other items. This is also true with respect to items sold by weight. For instance, we repack sugar into half kilo bags from a 50 kilos sack but our customers will request that we will divide this small bags further into 100 grams each or less. A laundry bar also ends being cut into ten or twelve, depending on the need of the requesting buyer. It has been their funny habit of visiting the store daily and to buy the same items in small retail sizes. Perhaps this has something to do with their budget or simply because they just want to go somewhere before they start their daily chores. To partially address this morning rush, we used small plastic tube bags intended for ice candy to repack cooking oils, kerosene, sugar and salt. But some still request to buy only a half of each small ice candy bags!

At that time, our town has no electricity yet and radio and television were not yet a fad. In fact, modesty aside, we owned one of the only three television sets in town. The other one is owned by an aunt who had children working in the cities. The third TV was owned by the hospital to entertain doctors and nurses. Because of our town's dire condition of having no communication facilities and entertainment that is available for the public, our store also served as a news and entertainment center of the community. The older ladies took turns being the news anchors during

Paul Roderick. A. Ysmael

the morning rush and the younger ones served as their interactive audience, occasionally asking clarificatory questions or post opinions just like we do today in Facebook or twitter. As they wait for their turn to be served by our limited store staff of two persons and me, they talk about who has given birth recently, if there is a legitimate father or otherwise or if he if the baby is at least "recognized." Aside from gossips, they also break the sad news as to who in town just passed away then they shift to happier news as to who passed an exam, who migrated to Hawaii, who will offer a free weekend lunch as a birthday celebrant or who will be marrying soon. They also talk about the funny and the bad things about their friends and neighbors. They share the gossip about neighborhood scandals and even about their favorite animals. If the news about the life of other is rare, they talk about ghosts and demons, sorcerers, fortune tellers and seers in town.

It is from our store that I learned the basics of business management. For instance, I learned how to determine the retail price for each item in order to avoid losses and earn modest profit without killing your market. I also learned supply management in my dealings with suppliers and human resource management from managing our two store workers. The fact that our store is now more than a century old, attests that I learned the basics right. I also learned about logistics. Our retailed items should not run short and should not also be overstocked. Because of the poor condition of the unpaved main road to the main Mac Arthur Highway that traverse coastal Ilocos, visitors then mockingly describe our main road as "a

Paul Roderick. A. Ysmael

dried riverbed rather than a road," where you need to spend five to six hours to travel a sixty kilometer stretch. A visit of a tropical storm will cut the town from the commercial centers of lowland Ilocos for several days. So for the store to continue serving the community, you need knowledge on logistics and inventory management. I also learned the fundamental of customer service and collection, which I think has helped me in my profession as a bank lawyer. As there have been numerous attempts by some neighbors to put up a competition but we were able to "maintain our market" until today my business course from our little store is my "MBA." So each time I have an opportunity of sharing my knowledge in business administration, I always make a reference to our sari-sari store.

However, this book is not about the basic skills in management and business. It is also about the stories that I learned from this store-- the rural legend about Yamashita's Trucks of Treasures. Each time that a farmer shares his difficulties in life over a glass of gin or the local basi, his drinking buddies and passing friends will always tell him to look for the remnants of Yamashita's "trucks of treasures" to ease his financial burden. And after such remark, the recurring tales of gold bars and bullions discovered beneath the trees, under the bridges, drinking springs and other places near the Yamashita escape route from Bessang Pass towards the Mountain Province will again be retold until all the bottles are emptied. Perhaps, the thought of discovering a piece of such treasure is brought into each of their drunken dreams that never will they forget about it. The tales of the

Paul Roderick. A. Ysmael

Yamashita treasure is part of each of the folks' youth and aging in this very idle town. It is a bedtime story for the young and a spirited conversation among the old who are allowed to drink. It is a tale that each of us in Cervantes heard of, but never took it as a serious matter. I was already a lawyer practicing my profession in Metro Manila when I met an old businessman who after finding that I come from Cervantes, asked me about Yamashita's trucks of treasures. I was surprised why he knew about it. He gave me a map where the said trucks may have passed but misplaced it in my office. What triggered my curiosity is the fact that this businessman is not from my old town but a self-confessed treasure hunter who is now overtaken by his age. He said that Yamashita's trucks of treasure was his dream treasure find but his business suffered a reversal to the point that he can no longer afford the expenses for such a treasure hunt. As I tried to recall where I misplaced his map, I also tried to remember what the story of Yamashita's trucks of treasures is all about.

    To appreciate this story further, please allow me to introduce you to the Gran Cordillera region where General Tomoyuki Yamashita hid during the last days of his Philippines that extends from the Province of Pangasinan in the south to Cagayan Valley in the north. It is located at the center of the island of Luzon and bounded by the provinces of Nueva Vizcaya and Isabela in the east and the long La Union and Ilocos coast in the west. Inside the heart of Cordillera are the provinces of Benguet, Mountain province, Kalinga, Apayao, Abra and Ifugao with some Ilocos towns like Cervantes and Quirino towns. The provinces and

Paul Roderick. A. Ysmael

towns inside the Cordillera are connected by narrow trails and at the time of war, were mostly unpaved and closed during rainy days. The first Ilocos town that is technically inside the Cordillera region is Cervantes. You can access Cervantes only by passing through a narrow pass beneath a mountain cut into two called the Bessang Pass. Until today, the Bessang Pass, located at the peak of a hill with an elevation of more than two thousand feet and characterized by thick pine forest and mossy rocks is the only access to Cordillera from the west coast unless you will try the more circuitous route in Abra or Ilocos Norte which at that time will cost you about three or four days more before you can hide in the Cordillera's vast forest heartland. So it was really expected of General Tomoyuki Yamashita to use Bessang Pass as his escape route. It is quicker for him to reach the pine forest mountains and the Pass is very strategic for him as it overlooks the whole Ilocos coast.

It was believed that when Yamashita retreated northwards, he had with him tons of treasures that are part of what the Japanese hoarded from the ancient temples of Asia's mainland which were temporarily stored in Fort Santiago in Manila. I could have done a geographic and chronological narration of how the treasures were transported but I opted to center my story in the heart of Cordillera, as a tribute to its own treasures and whom destiny decided to be the ultimate destination of Yamashita's Trucks of Treasures. As it is a tale, I believe that this story is purely fiction. Any similarity of the names of real people who are used in this story is purely incidental and should be considered as un-intentional. If it

Paul Roderick. A. Ysmael

contributes to the greatness of the names of those who passed away, perhaps it is my tribute to their good lives. In case however this story offends any feeling or memory of the dead or the reputation of the living, my apologies. My intention is to tell a story and not to hurt anyone.

Paul Roderick. A. Ysmael

Chapter One: The Attack

Poblacion, Cervantes, Ilocos Sur, February 15, 1945, 3:00 AM. The Cervantes Town Plaza was still asleep. The pitch black darkness courtesy of the Siberian fog greatly contributed to its deep slumber. Silence took this opportunity to conquer the cold midnight and extended its dominance until this dawning of a new morning. Not a single cock attempted to crow to bother the creeping conqueror. The green eagle owl standing on the branch of an old pine tree, its post for the last five years, yawned and stretched its wings in a manner so mild, to avoid producing any sound. The wisdom of this old wise bird is unable to fathom the placid domination of darkness over the light of dawn. The sage bird was so scared of the deafening silence to the point that it never attempted to hoot. The psychological noise created by the silence was really overwhelming. Even the belfry of the centuries-old baroque church failed to make any clatter. It moved its bells sans the chimes. The oppressing quiet however failed to deny the height of the belfry. Despite the darkness, the old tower of stone, egg white and clay is still clearly seen even from a mile by a sleepy human eye. The bell tower stood tall above all human made structures and even over acacia trees. It seems that even in darkness the aging structure is intently observing the decaying remnants of this old Spanish colonial settlement.

This town was once the capital of the sub-province of Amburayan and a bustling commercial center of this part of the country. Traders from the mountain towns of Abra, Bontoc and Benguet traded with their clients from the lowland cities of Ciudad Fernandina in Ilocos Sur and the port City of San Fernando in La Union. The lowland traders bartered to them the finest silk from China and the softest "abel" fabrics of Bangar and Vigan. Sometimes, the lowlanders bring with them china wares and clay pots or "burnay" from Vigan or the best cigars of Candon. They also bring seafood and other marine products in exchange for the best produce of the Cordillera-- gold, coffee and mountain vegetables.

Populated by less than five thousand settlers at that time, Cervantes is a typical agricultural town with "feudal" social structure. The elite of the society are identified by their large houses near the "poblacion." These rich families maintained "provincial ancestral

Paul Roderick. A. Ysmael

homes" while living somewhere in Ciudad Fernandina (Vigan) or in Manila. They are the landowners and the traders of the town. The farm caretakers, rice millers and sari-sari store owners composed the small middle class. Majority of the population are the mass of farmers, sugarcane planters and basi brewers. At the mountain areas, there are natives producing all types of vegetables, peanuts, root crop and handicrafts.

Prior to the coming of the Ilocano settlers, the town area was a fertile river delta sandwiched by the two branches of the Gran Cordillera Mountain Range. The first branch is the Benguet-La Union ridge and the other branch is the Abra-Montain Province Ridge. The two branches of the Cordilleras provide a romantic blue mountain panorama for either a sunrise or a sunset. The rays of the sun in the morning and in the afternoon clothed the town with golden rays in the first minute of day until the last second before twilight. This makes the town a green scenic valley with golden edges on either of its eastern or western sides, depending on what time of the day. The sun baked the fertile earth of the river delta which is naturally irrigated by two rivers, the Grand Amburayan Rio or the Abra River and the Cervantes River. The first river comes from the creeks and falls of the mountain provinces and Cervantes River is a collection of all waters that emanates from various creeks, watersheds of Mt. Namandirann and from the enticingly beautiful *Gambang Falls.*

The falls, fittingly considered as the town's jewel, is one of the most beautiful waterfalls in the country. It is known for its crystal clear showering waters that

Paul Roderick. A. Ysmael

fall into a natural water pool nestled in a rock cauldron. Aside from its fresh water resources, Cervantes is the only place in the Ilocos Region that has thick pine tree vegetation on scenic mountain formations that protect the town from typhoon. Hidden by mountains and covered by pine forests, the town, aside from being a trading center, was also an ideal hunting destination of Ilocano hunters. Its strategic location was noted by the Japanese Imperial forces commander who made the town as their resting station during their campaign in the Cordilleras. It is now the location of their logistics and medical camp in their retreat towards the Cordillera hinterlands all the way to the eastern coast of Luzon.

It is believed that this town settlement was founded by Ilocano hunters who decided to venture into limited agriculture in the area after recognizing the potential of its fertile land. Exchanging their hunting tools for hectares of land from the ethnic Igorot clans who once occupied the plains, they began transforming the grassland delta into rice fields. Another version of the town's origin is that it was an "encomienda" built by the Spanish friars. When the friars started their mission in the mountainous areas to Christianize the Igorot tribes, they got with them several meztizos from Vigan and from other lowland towns. After finding that the land here is more fertile than the coastal areas for various types of plants and fruit trees, these meztizos, with the blessings of the friars, converted the plains into their haciendas. By that time, Cervantes has two cattle ranches owned by Spanish mestizos and three major rice haciendas. The main settlement is composed of three barrios, the

Paul Roderick. A. Ysmael

names of these barrios--Rosario, San Juan and Concepcion-- prove that they are Catholic Settlements. Until now, these three barrios are where the hardworking migrant Ilocanos, known for their skill as rice planters and appetite for professional education, live. They work in the Tamaang Plains, a valley of about one hundred hectares of fertile agricultural land irrigated by three shallow creeks and several springs. Because of its topography and rich soil, the plains are devoted to rice and tropical vegetables. The Tamaang Plains is owned by not more than four families either of Spanish or Chinese descent. Around the plains are several sugarcane, corn and peanuts (mountain legume) plantations that complement the rice production. Cervantes produces rice, muscovado sugar, corn, "achuete" and even black pepper which they sell to the mountain settlements of Mankayan and Buguias in Benguet and in Bauko and Bontoc in the Mountain Province. The quaint town also produces until now, oranges and avocado on a limited scale, the local endemic Cervantes Red Cherry ("sirali"), peanuts, star apple, mangoes, cane sugar and the legendary Cervantes rice. From the creeks and rivers, they got the famed and sumptuous West Cordillera mountain eel, which is regarded as source of strength and long life. From hunting activities, they have dried wild boar and deer meat. The local produce is traded with the products and wares of the visiting traders. Its two ranches produce the dairy requirement of the town and some native chicken and pigs are available at the backyard pens of the farmers. The sugarcane planters also brew their own version of the "basi," rum made from fermented molasses and also ferment their own Ilocos vinegar. Their "basi" and vinegar are believed to

Paul Roderick. A. Ysmael

be much better than what the lowlands produce because of their better sugar cane variety and a more fertile land. Cervantes at that time is a flourishing agricultural and commercial town. Traders and artisans visited once in a while offering their non-agricultural products like farming equipment, all kinds of tools, oil lamps and clothing apparel. It had two bakeries that had the tasty pan de sal and a hardware store owned by Pay Kim Sim, a wealthy Chinese migrant who monopolized the trading of steel, cement and machineries, including fertilizers and oil. A major street is now named in his honor.

The Market Place located beside the Old Town Hotel is still bustling with various goods ranging from Chinese dinnerware and lanterns from La Union, "abel" fabric and bed sheets, tobacco and garlic from Ciudad Fernandina, wooden furniture, knives and tools from Candon and other towns, coffee and rice from Bontoc and gold and vegetables of all kinds from Benguet. By all indications, Cervantes was the wealthiest town in the Cordillera region at the time next only to the capital town of La Trinidad and Baguio City. It has a relatively large middle class population as evidenced by large houses with names of professionals placed on its walls, evidencing its high literacy rate.

Typical of any Spanish colonial settlement, the Church and the Catholic School are located at the eastern portion of the central quadrangle. Across them are the Municipal Town Hall and the Public School and between them is a park, a marketplace and the once romantic Old Town Hotel. The Southern side of

Paul Roderick. A. Ysmael

the Plaza is the Gabaldon, which used to house the "guardia civil and the residence of the Spanish military commander of the whole Amburayan Province.

During the First and early part of Second World War, the town enjoyed relative peace and prosperity because of its relative distance from Manila and major cities. This peace was shattered when the Japanese arrived. The Japanese occupation caused unimaginable sufferings to suspected guerilla fighters and their families because of the various forms of wicked interrogation practices that included tortures and rapes, that instilled fear and depression among the cheerful settlers.

The old colonial hotel is now a garrison and home for around a thousand Japanese Imperial Soldiers composed of Japanese natives and fierce Korean conscripts, the Gabaldon, is now a Protestant Church where American missionaries used to occupy before they were attacked by the Japanese, ten of them killed, five captured and are still detained there until this time. The remaining two who managed to evade arrest and are with the Filipino guerrillas serving as spiritual counselors. The brick and mortar town hall, with its "balconahe" proudly displaying Japanese Imperial and military flags, is now the seat of the Japanese-installed municipal government. It is manned by a puppet mayor and guarded by more than a hundred Makapilis, serving as municipal constabulary and police force. The Japanese-founded the Makapilis as their auxiliary constabulary force to replace policemen who were loyal to the Commonwealth Government. These Makapilis served

Paul Roderick. A. Ysmael

as their spies for alleged traitors against the Japanese rule. Much of the sufferings and torture during the war were attributed to the reports of the Makapilis who were allegedly using their positions to avenge their personal grudges against their fellow Filipinos. They were the most maligned and hated persons in the Philippine society during and after the war.

Despite the raging Second World War, only the occasional attacks against the garrison by guerrillas led by a Filipino-Spanish Cervantes resident can be claimed as the town's contribution to the international strife. Cervantes was still a major trading and agricultural town in this part of the war-torn archipelago. The townsfolk were generally unmindful of the result of the Pacific war and busied themselves with their daily chores of tilling their lands and tending their livestock. Their attitude towards the war was understandable considering that the town is 350 kilometers away from Manila and 130 kilometers away from Baguio City. But tonight, the town will contribute more than shooting skirmishes to the war. It will define the outcome of the bloodiest jungle battle of World War II--the Battle of Bessang Pass.

With the moon at its slimmest crescent and the thick fog descending from the Cordilleras is at its thickest volume, darkness and silence conspired to cloak the events that slowly unfolded in this appointed dawn. Two Japanese sentries are now both restive and drowsy. They are on their fourth hour of their guarding shift and there attentiveness is suspect. They tried to evade sleeping by sipping a hot coffee from their tin cups. The caffeine, despite filling their veins

Paul Roderick. A. Ysmael

with energy, however is having a difficult bout with the fatigue that their bodies have been enduring for the past nights of standing nearly four full hours. Coupled by the silence and coolness of the night, their bodies are being constrained by their fatigue to have a nap. This is shown by their intermittent yawning and stretching. The first sentry is Sgt. Toki Yamamoto, a 25 year-old conscript from Tokyo, Japan who took over from one of his men who claimed to have "been stricken of malaria." He arrived in the Philippines two years earlier to help his Emperor's campaign for the Great Asian Co-Prosperity Sphere, which actually means, conquest of the whole Asia under the Japanese Imperial Rule. Young, tall and athletic, he was assigned to the 73rd Tora (Tiger) Division of the Japanese Imperial Army which served as the buffer guard of General Tomoyuki Yamashita known for its fierce Korean conscripts. He served as a Military Police or MP guarding the garrisons occupied by the Tora Division. He has learned to love the place and found love amidst the raging war. With the rugged but gentle mountainous landscape of pine forests, the town of Cervantes reminded him of the rural areas of northern Japan *sans* the icy peaks and the sweet sushi. The topography and climate eased his homesickness unlike the warm and purely tropical climate of Manila where he served his first six months guarding Fort Santiago. Here in the Cervantes Garrison, there may be no glistening ice cap and sweet sushi but it is in this garrison that he saw the shining beauty and felt the sweetness of a fair complexioned local laundry girl, Benita Langbay. She may not have the beauty that a kimono clads in his native Japan but she had the smile that can even dim even the glaring ray of the

Paul Roderick. A. Ysmael

rising sun. Her petite but commanding portrait helped erased the sadness of this lonely soldier, fighting a losing war, miles away from home. Their story may not fit in this war-torn time but beneath the firing guns and burning violence, theirs was love which truly existed despite the patriotic hatred that divided their national allegiances.

Likewise tall at five feet and ten inches is his buddy, Tomo Yamazaki, born in San Francisco, USA of Japanese parents, they were able to flee the United States and settled in the Philippines just after the bombing of Pearl Harbor. American in upbringing but Japanese by heart, his father was recruited to serve the Japanese Occupation Forces as a cook in their main camp in Fort Santiago. This paved the way for the son to join the Tora Division which successfully drove away Gen. Douglas Mac Arthur and his forces from the island of Corregidor into his short and temporary exile in Australia. Tomo always bragged that he was the one who personally arrested and handcuffed the arms of the surrendering American commander, General King about three years earlier in that island fortress, west of Manila. He was transferred to the MP Division with a rank of a corporal to provide muscle to the men who would ensure that the Koreans in their fold will be loyal to the Emperor.

As he finished his cup of coffee, Toki spread his eyes towards the "municipio" or town hall building across the main "poblacion" road where he saw four (4) Filipino "Makapilis," probably talking about the raging battle in the nearby Buccual Ridge, the Western Tip of the Gran Cordillera Mountain Ranges. The Makapili

Paul Roderick. A. Ysmael

leader, Badong Buguas, a native of Barrio Malaya is pointing at the top of the ridge. Buguas seemed to be confident that the Bessang Pass can never be conquered. The Makapilis' blind trust and confidence on their Japanese master's might and position, have bolstered their own ruthless abuses against the suspected relatives of Filipino guerillas who sided with the former United States Armed Forces in the Far East or USAFFE. Unknown to them the fledging guerilla forces in the Cordillera are now joined by several hundreds of escapees of the Bataan Death March and Ilocano evacuees who had nothing to do other than to fight. With additional forces and veteran trainors, they now call themselves United States Forces in the Philippines-Northern Luzon or USAFIP-NL.

Toki then motioned Tomo Yamazaki to look at the back of the garrison building as he sat down on the floor. Convinced that everything was alright, Toki relaxed himself and leaned towards the wall. Perhaps, he was only about ten seconds into sleeping when he heard a gunshot from Tomo's rifle. He scrambled to stand up and ran towards Tomo who was still firing and loading his rifle relentlessly aimed at the garrison's ammunition depot which is now razing with fire. Around a hundred Japanese soldiers were already firing at the same direction. At his peripheral vision he saw the old green eagle owl in scampering flight away from the blazing bullets. Toki saw shadows of small men running away from the garrison, two were about to throw gasoline containers towards the fire. He aimed his rifle towards the two men's direction but two shots were fired ahead of him towards his direction. He docked and lied low as two bullets passed around

Paul Roderick. A. Ysmael

three inches above his abdomen. He fired back to prevent the shooter from further pursuing him. As he looked up, he saw the shooter in a fast retreat, but the loaded rifle is still pointed towards him. He fired successively but the shooter opted to run rather than to shoot back. He knelt with his rifle butt mounted on his right chest and fired all the remaining bullets of his ammo clip towards the direction of the running assailant but he knew he only managed to hit at the darkness.

At last, the rule of silence ended and the darkness was bumped off by the flames of the burning ammunition depot. Shots were exchanged, the machinegun at the sentry tower went in full battle sound aimed at every position the enemies may be located. Toki, now squatting behind the concrete wall at the stairway was able to aim his rifle to a moving object camouflaged by a green blanket, he got a nice shot and the guerilla was down. He put another bullet into the guerilla's head to ensure he was dead. In a matter of a minute, the fire was put off, the Makapilis were able to make one arrest and picked one dead. Around three hundred Japanese soldiers are now up on their feet, the noise of their rowdy scamper finally defeated the conquest of silence. Not contented with their failed pursuit the Japanese soldiers fired mortars towards the escaping guerillas but the attack was well-planned and systematic. The attackers did not come to wage a shooting battle, they just came to announce their presence and left.

Col. Makoto Moha, the Japanese Garrison Commander was fuming mad. He was ranting at the

Paul Roderick. A. Ysmael

Makapilis who once again failed to guard the perimeter of the garrison while praising Tomo and Toki for their alertness and capability to stop the burning of the depot. It was his instruction that the local constabulary force called the Makapilis will conduct perimeter patrols. This was Moha's effective strategy of minimizing the exposure of the Japanese soldiers and the abusive Korean conscripts to the local populace and to dispel the impression that they are an "invasion" force. This approach has gained him relative acceptance and popularity from the locals. He learned this from his commander in Korea when he was still a battalion commander and a young captain. Because of the laxity of the of the Makapili patrol, he ordered an investigation if there are Makapilis who are treacherously aiding the guerillas. He now suspects that there have been several spies going in and out of the garrison. First in his list aside from the arrested Alberto Fungway are the laundrywomen who even maintained romantic relationships with some of his men. He suspects that some of these women may have been guerilla spies. He however did not know that Toki is one of those who were having an affair with a beautiful local lass working as a laundrywoman and indeed she was likewise a guerilla spy. A nurse by profession, Benita worked in the Philippine Army medical corps before she was recruited by Albert Fungway to join the intelligence command, capitalizing on her ethnic charms and beautiful face, she was always assigned by Fungway as his lone advance reconnaissance force in his various missions. This time she arrived a year before Fungway was ever seen in Cervantes. Benita disguised as a poor orphan mountain lass applying as laundrywoman to the

Paul Roderick. A. Ysmael

town's middle class until she joined the laundrywomen who were washing the uniform of the soldiers in the garrison. Benita had always avoided having any romantic liaisons with her subjects, but the young and mild-mannered Toki, earned her affection as he always expressed his care to her every time she set foot inside the garrison. Her admiration ripened to affection until true love bloomed from their daily interaction.

Moha finally ordered his young administrative officer, Lt. Yumi Yamaha to prepare an assessment of the attack in order to fortify the garrison's defenses. Before returning to his quarters, Moha glanced at the ammo depot, shaking his head as he began to walk.

Paul Roderick. A. Ysmael

Chapter Two: The Bolo Men

Anacleto Octaviano is an Ilocano native who joined the guerrilla front in his early a teens because he has nothing else to do. Born in Cervantes, Ilocos Sur of landed parents who both died of cholera when he was still a baby, he was raised like his own son by his grandfather Angkay Elmo, a former farmer who managed to carve-out farmlands from silted riverbanks and hills to become a small landowner of less than thirty hectares of land. Privileged of bounty harvests and over-protective care from his grandfather, Anacleto did not feel the need to study nor work in the farm. They had farm workers to ensure the good

Paul Roderick. A. Ysmael

harvest and he had his grandfather to ensure his future. His early teenage years were mostly spent in the Plaza, joining the affluent mestizo sons of Spanish families playing ping pong and joining them in their nightly dancing at the cabarets, until the cabarets were closed by the imperial army in order to please the wives of their customers and to abide by the request of the Catholic parish priest. Lacking anything to do, most of the cabaret-dancing men opted to just join the guerilla force rather than being suspected of being guerilla sympathizers by the Makapilis. Young men of their age, dreaded the Korean conscripts led by a certain Tae-pon Doung-yi, a huge Korean with a devil's smile who was both an expert in water torture and an enthusiast of the Russian roulette.

So, just like the bored and restless mestizos, Anacleto joined a ragtag guerilla force led by a scion of the Spanish Family who owns the Hacienda Moreno in the southern plains of the town, named Angel Moreno. Moreno's assistant is a former high school PMT commander, Carlitos Leiza, and they respectively assumed the ranks of First and Second Lieutenant with the blessing of the main guerilla commander, Col. Volckman. Short for his four-foot and ten inches, height and skinny frame, Anacleto was not qualified to join the regular platoon. Instead, he was assigned to the Philippine version of the "terra-cotta warriors," the battalion sized commandoes called the "the bolo men."

Armed only with home-made knives, Chinese machetes and Batangas-made bolos this "rag-tag force" of short Ilocano natives and Igorots also carry sharpened bamboo poles of about four feet long to

Paul Roderick. A. Ysmael

resemble rifles during the night. The "bolo men" played the parts of both a bluffing army and an auxiliary force. During the night, with their lighted torch carried by their leader, they march in platoon formation with their bamboo poles on their shoulders, creating a silhouette of marching riflemen. The bamboo poles have sharpened edges that can be used to stab the Japanese and its other end has clothes soaked in kerosene and are lighted to torch garrisons or homes that are aiding the Japanese forces. The name "bolo men" was either due to the fact that these men are armed only with bolos or because the specie of the bamboo that they used is called "bulo" in Ilocano or "buhu" in Tagalog. Whatever the source of their band's name, however, this tactic of letting them carry the bamboo poles especially at night, psychologically aided the real armed Filipino and American soldiers by increasing their numbers in the eyes of the enemy. Far from just being "terra cottas," however, the bolomen are real living soldiers, perhaps even better and braver than members of the regular guerilla army. They fight in close encounters, gaining expertise, due to the necessity of survival, in knife to knife combat and martial arts. They were instrumental in transporting to the guerilla fronts, arms and ammunition unloaded by American submarines in Northern Luzon during the Japanese Occupation. The bolomen set up booby traps used in numerous ambush attacks against the travelling Japanese Mobile Regiment. They attacked and raze down garrisons, ammunition depots, Imperial Japanese granaries, houses of suspected Japanese supporters. They also made arrests of suspected traitors. They were paid by the promise of liberation, a pack of "20's Lucky Seven" and by imported canned

Paul Roderick. A. Ysmael

goods, candies and chocolates which they gave to their wives and children. By the end of World War II, the bolomen in Northern Luzon reached a peak of around twenty thousand divided into ten command posts scattered from Tarlac in the south to Tuguegarao in the North, even the northernmost island of Batanes has a recorded presence of these warriors.

Barely twenty-two and had no formal education, Anacleto did not have the profile of a revolutionary. He just followed his friends. Unfortunately, his mestizo friends were assigned at the regular guerilla force while he was assigned to the bolomen force. The mestizos were able to insert themselves in the regular guerilla army not only because of their height. Other reasons are their blood lineage, their having their own hunting rifles and American pistols or even old muskets. Anacleto, the short native who only had an old Swiss knife was not at their class. He was however assigned to the "elite" bolomen regiment under Artemio Miranda, a native of Piddig, Ilocos Norte who was operating in the hinterlands of Abra and the Cordilleras. Having a scattered force of around a thousand men, Miranda claimed the rank of colonel and so he was recognized as such even by the regular US and Filipino armed forces, making him a de facto officer of the USAFFIP-NL.

In as much as he was not sure of what he was doing, Anacleto was not also aware on the importance of their mission on that midnight of February 14, 1945. He was asked by his troop commander to go back to the camp of 2nd Lt. Carlitos Leiza, his town mate and recruiter, just a day before the attack. His

Paul Roderick. A. Ysmael

assignment is to enter the small window leading to the office of the garrison commander and get a newly received package contained in a box. Leiza was supposed to lead two squads of both bolomen and regular fighters in the attack. He himself was not aware of the objectives but they were supposed to hand over the box to a guerilla officer named "Ferdinand Marcos" operating under a guerilla **nom de guer** of "Marcial Esguerra," an Ilocano lawyer whom Leiza met in Manila during their ROTC days before the war and whom he cannot refuse for personal reasons. This story about the "independent" guerilla force led by Esguerra or whom other guerilla leaders claim to be Marcos has been verified by the USAFIP-NL officers who allowed him to operate in the area for a "special mission" under direct orders from General Romulo and the Philippine High Command. With the permission from his direct superior, Lt. Angel Moreno, Leiza agreed to lead the mission to "recover" something from the Japanese garrison. On Esguerra's instruction, they should prioritize the recovery and avoid engaging the enemy.

So they met at the mouth of Amburayan River Delta behind the old church. Disguised as charcoal vendors, they went around the plaza and surveyed the garrison. They then agreed on each other's specific tasks for that raid. They inventoried their arms and tools. They simulated the execution of their mission ten times to attain precision. They familiarized with each others' voice, size and mannerisms to ensure that they can effectively coordinate with each other under the dark. They divided themselves as agreed under their leaders and major players—2nd Lt. Leiza, Albert

Paul Roderick. A. Ysmael

Fungway, an Igorot from Bontoc and a regular guerilla officer and Gurod Kiblongan is an Igorot from Cervantes, he is the leader of the bolomen contingent of seven including Anacleto. Fungway will lead the six bolomen inside the garrison compound to set the ammunition depot on fire, create distraction and leave. Leiza will lead the other team to secure Anacleto as he steals the package inside the Garrison Commander's office. They may shoot at the Japanese to cover his exit only if necessary. Otherwise, they were under strict orders not to fire and just exit immediately and leave the garrison. They should ignore any opportunity to harm the enemy, the package is more than an enemy's life and the recovery of the same is primordial.

The attack was executed as planned, they were able to penetrate the garrison at around midnight. Incidentally, but part of the intelligence component of the mission, the Japanese had a Valentine's Party the night before, where ladies of the town were invited to dance with the soldiers. Alcohol and opium were abundant during the night that explains the deep slumber of the soldiers and the limited number of sentries who were awake. Toki, who neither drinks nor smoke was forced to take over the post of his man because the sentry was high with opium. The garrison then was really vulnerable to an attack. The Japanese relied on the Makapilis too much not knowing that their Filipino cohorts are as complacent and lax even more than the proverbial "complacent proud rabbit which lost to a turtle in a race."

True enough only a person the size of Anacleto can enter the small ventilation below the porch leading

Paul Roderick. A. Ysmael

to the office. As soon as Anacleto entered the ventilation, Kiblongan lit the gasoline-dipped torch with his match and threw it inside the ammo depot. There were cracking like firecrackers and then a loud bang which scattered several rifles to the ground. The scattered rifles distracted Kiblongan so much. Tempted to get a rifle of his own Kiblongan, under a green blanket camouflage, ran towards the door of the depot. It was there where he met the bullets of Toki. As Fungway attempted to rescue him he was arrested by the platoon of responding Makapilis, which he managed to shoot three. Except of that tragedy, the diversion worked effectively, Anacleto, Leiza and the ten others successfully evaded capture and they got the package. They left the place as fast as they could, securing the package. They were unmindful of their dead comrade and captured leader, as if somebody else would take care of them. For Kiblongan, he lost his life in the said raid but a barrio near Bessang Pass will be named after him, ten years later. This successful mission changed Anacleto's role in the war and his perspective in life.

Paul Roderick. A. Ysmael

Chapter Three: Albert Fungway

Albert Fungway is the typical career soldier. Tall at five feet and eight inches, medium built with dark skin that is tanned by the warm climate of Bontoc, Mt. Province, this young man really wanted to be a soldier. His father was a miner and his mother was a coffee vendor. He studied high school at the protestant Mission School.. He graduated from the Baguio Military Institute in Irisan, Baguio City and finished the Officer's Course at Fort Mc Kinley in Manila. He was commissioned as officer to the Commonwealth Army in 1940, just before the war broke out. After a successful stint in the island of Mindanao as a marine officer, guarding a fort in Zamboanga City from pirates, he was assigned to the Army Intelligence Service. He proved his prowess in intelligence service when in 1943, he discovered the huge shipment of heavy armor and artillery, modern naval weaponry, arms and ammunition in the Cavite area as preparatory to the Japanese Invasion of the Philippines. The landing of the large naval weaponry and arms cache contributed to the decision of the American Asiatic Fleet to withdraw from Manila Bay to Java, Indonesia in the following year to avoid severe damages. It was said that the American Command ignored his report. When he was posted in the Cordilleras, he was the most senior Filipino intelligence officer in the area. Operating in his native terrain, he was effective in gathering vital tactical information for the Cordillera campaign dubbed as "Oplan Big Bounty." Fungway has been operating in

Paul Roderick. A. Ysmael

the area since General Yamashita took refuge in the hinterlands of the Cordilleras. His mission was to track the Yamashita trail, estimate its size, evaluate its firepower and coordinate his intelligence information to the American forces in the area under Colonel Volkmann.

When the US and Filipino Forces learned of the strong blocking force stationed in Cervantes, he was sent to verify the report. Reaching Cervantes via backdoor through Ifugao and Bontoc, his cover was being a coffee vendor supplying the landed elites of Cervantes and the neighboring towns. Of course, he made contact to the local guerilla forces. He then supplied coffee to the Japanese appointed mayor of Cervantes town after being introduced to him by a clandestine guerilla financier, named Cirilo Gadiano Ysmael, who acted as his "coffee retailer" and protector. A month prior to the attack, Fungway was already selling coffee to Col. Moha, who favored his "alamid" or civet cat coffee, the most expensive and aromatic coffee in the world. The civet cat coffee is brewed from coffee beans swallowed and then secreted by civet cats. It is believed that the civet cat only eats the best-tasting beans of a coffee tree and the chemicals in its stomach and intestines, transform the beans into the best tasting coffee beans on Earth. Farmers will soon pick the civet cat's dung every morning. They will clean them with pure spring water, dry them under the tropical sun and roast them with fire of burning pine tree sticks. The bean will also capture the mint of the pine tree creating its unique aromatic taste that is only found in the Cordilleras.

Paul Roderick. A. Ysmael

Col. Moha was so enamored to Fungway's alamid coffee that he allowed Fungway to stay in his office room while he is receiving instructions from his Japanese superiors. Unknown in this side of historical past, Fungway's friendship with Col. Moha was instrumental in the weakening of the imperial forces in the Cordillera as he overheard many instructions which, as a trained intelligence officer, has understood, noted and reported them to his superiors. Aside from confirming the existence of the "package" inside the office of Moha, he was able to hear conversations and see several papers of strategic importance every time that he gets an opportunity to eavesdrop on conversations and peek at the papers. He also had an "insider's view" on the garrison and gained familiarity with the structure and people inside.

Albert Fungway expected it, when he was arrested resisting his captors and after killing three Filipino Makapilis, his rights as a prisoner of war were forgotten. Two tall and lanky Koreans were assigned to give him the physical ritual of torture that he never experienced nor witnessed in his entire military life.

To prepare for any eventuality, veteran guerillas who attack garrisons avoid water for three days. Their thirst will make the water torture to them as luxury, at least for the first three galloons. Hence, Fungway's dehydrated and thirsty body welcomed the water torture as it swallowed the first three galloons of water with ease, even the Koreans were stunned to witness how their victim seemed to enjoy the water being poured into his mouth. But the surprised Koreans had no time for any delay, Fungway then felt the pain of

Paul Roderick. A. Ysmael

rifle buts all over his back. The Koreans were not talking, they are just hitting him of anything they can pick, first the rifles, then a steel pipe, a shovel, a wrecked chair and then the final five galloons of water that went out from his mouth, ears and even from his anus. He lost consciousness. After few minutes, the Makapilis took their turn of beating him. He was being asked in the vernacular about the attack while being hit, they demanded his ":real" name and their leader's name. They asked about their hideout. Fungway pretended to be confused and frightened. He just gave his tormentors a blank stare as he as he was thinking for his next moves. Then he was out again.

As he was dragged into his cell, badly beaten by the Makapilis, Fungway vividly recalled the success of their operation to recover the package. He was the only person shooting back at the Japanese and Koreans who trooped to defend their depot and unmindful of Anacleto's entry into the garrison commander's den. In fact he could have escaped if not for Kiblongan, who wanted to grab a rifle. He decided to recover Kiblongan because he feared he was still alive and he might tell the truth when tortured and be killed slowly. If only he saw the second bullet that hit Kiblongan's head, he could have backed out and just reported a casualty. Now, he is preparing for the second round of torture. He realized however that even the soldiers were not aware of the importance of the documents that they were able to seize. In fact this also gave him doubts as to the value of the package that they stole. If the package was that valuable, a sentry could have been assigned to guard it the whole night. On the contrary, his other brain is arguing that it may be of absolute

Paul Roderick. A. Ysmael

confidentiality that even the Japanese soldiers should not know. Whatever it is, however, they succeeded in getting it, just like how they were successful in gathering information about the enemy. He observed however that there were only about three hundred soldiers in this garrison that is supposed to be a camp for 5,000 men. As an intelligence officer, he knows that the Japanese Command had deployed its troops somewhere. He took note also of the fact that the armory seemed to be containing a limited number of ammunition. This means that the deployment is not for patrol but intended for heavy battle. Contrary to their impression that the garrison is a hospital area, it had only a clinic and few medics. There are only about twenty wounded soldiers who are recovering from their injuries ranging from amputated leg to blinded eyes. This means that the Japanese are preparing to abandon this place.

He was in this state of mind when he felt a pain in his right thumb. The Makapili is using a large needle to prick it. As Fungway just stared at him, the Makapili slapped him on both sides of his face. "Wake up, coffee cowboy!" and he felt pain at his belly as the knee of the Makapili hit it twice. He spread his eyes around the place.

If only looks can slice a person, Moha's eyes already made a ground meat out of his muscles and powder out of his bones. Moha felt betrayed and fooled. Only heaven knows how he can survive their second encounter. He then watched how the darkness faded into the light of a new day. He wiped his bloody

Paul Roderick. A. Ysmael

face by rubbing it on his shoulders, he made a deep gasp, then slept while hanged in chains.

Fungway had a deep slumber, he dreamt of having been shot in the Cervantes Town Plaza. He saw his friends jeering at him, calling him a traitor as he gasped for his last breath. As he fell, he saw a bright white light leading to a golden cloud where he was welcomed by an old man, smiling at him. Suddenly someone snatched him and he was being dragged to hell! He screamed. And he woke up as four Makapilis were already dragging his asleep body to the garrison interrogation dungeon.

Contrary to his preparation, Albert Fungway was met by a lady Japanese soldier who ordered Benita Langbay and another lady to clean his body and give him clean clothing. In crisp English with Japanese accent, the lady Japanese officer told him that upon orders of the commander, she will be treating him gently as there is a possibility that he was forcibly recruited by the guerillas. They know he is a stranger to Cervantes and that he has respected friends who even want to visit him. "The commander wants you to be pleasantly dressed when your friends arrive," said the lady officer. "However, please help us identify the leaders of the attackers. They took something valuable from us, which you may not know because you were with the diversionary group."

Fungway observed that the lady officer was sincere in her impression that he was forcibly recruited by the attackers. He began his story, "Madam, I was kidnapped by the attackers. They also got my daughter with them. If I will not cooperate, they

Paul Roderick. A. Ysmael

will kill her. I cannot identify anyone of them because they are using false names." He then glanced at Benita, who just gave him an empty stare as she continued cleaning his wounds and abrasions with soap and water, pretending to hear nothing.

"I am even afraid to talk about it, but I was forced of doing this..... You know that I am one of the close friends of Colonel Moha, if I have a choice, I will not do this thing but how can I betray my only child, and an innocent daughter as she is?"

"But you know where they are camping, where are they coming from?," the lady officer gently asked. He slowly moved his head sideways. Suddenly, someone kicked her from behind. He fell. Then he felt a whip hitting his swollen legs. He was again kicked and his head was forcibly raised. He saw the eyes of Moha just an inch above his forehead, as Moha shouted as he warded off Benita Lang-ay. "RIAR! RIAR! DO NOT FOOR US! I ROST A PACKAGE TODAY AND ONRI YOU HAS TO KNOW IT!"

"You are my friend Mr. Fungway but in the name of my Emperor, I WIRR KIRR YOU! PREASE ,,, cooperate!"

Fungway knows he had to give something. "They staged their operation inside the cave behind the old church, it is called the Cabaroan cave. They are keeping my daughter there, Madam."

"Okay, then," he heard Moha, "CREAN him again and dress him up, one of his friends will be

Paul Roderick. A. Ysmael

visiting him today.!" He gave Fungway a kick in the groin, which was the last beating that he suffered.

"Fungway, once I discover you are lying, I wirr shoot you myself!!!"

After cleaning Fungway, Benita Lang-ay gestured to bring out the basin of water and the towels that she used to clean the prisoner and casually left the place.

Paul Roderick. A. Ysmael

Yamashita's Trucks of Treasures

Chapter Four: The Rescue

Paul Roderick. A. Ysmael

Cirilo Gadiano Ysmael, a caretaker of a Spanish landlord and a farmer himself expected his regular guest in the late morning of February 15, 2011. His residence, one of the few two-storey houses in town, that also housed his convenience store, barn and his rice mill, are only half mile away from the garrison. With such distance, he heard both the gunshots and the news about the attack nearly at the same time. Then at thirty years old, tall at five feet and ten inches with a very muscular body, he is both a community leader and enforcer of order among the farmers. He is respected both by the landed elite and the poor farmers. His authority and network has a placed him in the town's social circle as liaison of the rich and the poor; the mediator between Japanese and the Filipino leaders; and unknown to the Imperial conquerors, a benefactor of the guerilla movement. Because of his stature in the local circle and the distance of his home and the garrison, his home is among the favorite places for breakfast of Colonel Moha. Cirilo knew that the Colonel maybe a little late because of the Valentine's Party that he organized the night before and the skirmishes that followed it at dawn.. He then asked his wife to prepare a breakfast for his regular guest. There is nothing special for this morning. There is the usual pan de sal from his Chinese friend's bakery, the brewed alamid coffee which was being freshly roasted while the guerillas were attacking the garrison, their home-made guava jam, smoked fish, pork adobo, fried rice and fresh carabao's milk, all are already served perpetually on his morning table. The difference for this morning is the presence of red-orange bananas called "udang" which are cultivated in the mountains by the Igorots and rarely reaches the

Paul Roderick. A. Ysmael

town center especially during the war as transporting them was made difficult by the raging battle in Bessang Pass.

     Colonel Moha with his two aides and a platoon of guards arrived at Cirilo's yard before nine in the morning. The guards surrounded the compound while the aides stayed at the gate. Only their commander will partake his breakfast with his host. Cirilo avoided any conversation on the attack and just greeted his guest with a bow and "Ohayo!" However, after his usual low bows of three, Moha shouted "Your friend Fungway helped the damned guerillas!" As he sat down, he repeated the news which Cirilo heard from the person who delivered his pan de sal. Interrupted only by his unusually fast gnawing of the bread and his favorite adobo, Moha hurled invectives and repeatedly expressed his disgust and hatred to Fungway and the Filipino "traitors." It seems that he did not even notice the unusual color of the banana being served before him, which color resembles his angry face. "But the danger is not that they got the armory on fire, my friend, they got some documents that are very important to the Imperial army," Moha blurted as he forgot that he was sharing intelligence information, "I cannot also imagine how he was so careless for a businessman that he allowed them to get his daughter!" Cirilo just pretended to be listening while thinking how can he help Fungway. There is no doubt that Fungway's life is in danger in the hands of the Korean conscripts. He has heard of several detained Filipinos who were released by Moha but later on found dead near the garrison for "trying to steal something." Cirilo know Fungway from head to

Paul Roderick. A. Ysmael

foot and vice versa. He is unmarried and never sired a child. He gestured to reach for water which the Japanese acceded with a nod. "You know Ciriro, I wirr miss your friendship when I get back to Japan. You are so kind to the Japanese here, I learned a lot from you, my friend. As a gesture of friendship I am giving to you my army knife, which I have used since joining the army for this war."[1]

Cirilo just smiled and accepted the knife exclaiming "Arigato, colonel Moha, me and my family will miss you too." Moha then went back to their topic.

"You know, I understand why Fungway was forced to lead those bastards into my office, I also have a daughter back in Japan, and just a thought that I may not be back there to see her gives me a big fear in my head!," he nodded his balding head once more, "I will try to rescue his daughter and free him this afternoon."

Cirilo then asked about the condition of Fungway. Learning that he is fine, he volunteered to talk to him and ask for more information. That ended the conversation. Moha finished his glass of water, greeted everybody that he saw in the house and left the place.

It was already around four in the afternoon when Cirilo went to the garrison. He was greeted by a Makapili who immediately sneered at his back as he passed by. Cirilo has long been suspected by the

---

[1] The said army knife was discovered by the author hidden in the old barn which is around five inches long and made of pure steel.

Paul Roderick. A. Ysmael

Makapilis as a guerilla collaborator. Carlitos Leiza, a notorious guerilla and a regular USAFIP-NL troop commander is his nephew, being a son of his sister. Of course, they cannot simply arrest him for being the uncle of a guerilla leader. Not to mention his friendship with the garrison commander and his influence with the landlords who are all supportive of Cirilo. The Makapilis have been working to look for an actual proof to substantiate their suspicion against Cirilo. They cannot wait for the time when they can have something to show to the Japanese authorities. The thrilling and very adverse relationship between Cirilo and the Makapilis, however, his is a different story.

    Upon reaching the compound of the garrison he observed that only around a hundred soldiers are present, and all are in high alert. He was met by the lady officer who interrogated Fungway. She smiled and introduced herself as Miko Sato, she used to work in the Japanese Embassy as information analyst while doubling as a Japanese intelligence officer. She then led Cirilo to the dungeon and informed him about the instructions of the garrison commander. He said that Fungway will be released to his care because the prisoner needs medical attention which they cannot provide because they are preparing the defense of the town against the possible advance of the American forces from Bessang Pass. Two Makapilis will be sent to guard Fungway in order to prevent his escape. She answered Cirilo's questions without even hearing what he was asking. Moha and his men went to "rescue" the daughter of Fungway who is being held captive by the guerillas encamped east of the town. As Cirilo knew

Paul Roderick. A. Ysmael

Fungway has never sired a child, he just nodded his head to conceal his relief that Moha believed Fungway's false story.

As she finished talking, the sounds of a firing mortar were heard east of the town followed by machine gun and rifle fire. It seems however that the shots and the firing are coming from one direction and are all aimed towards the cave near the cemetery. It is just about two kilometers east of the garrison. Cirilo silently prayed for the safety of the "child" being rescued.

With the rattling gunshots at the background, Cirilo cursed Fungway in his booming voice and scolded him for betraying Moha and their Japanese friends. The sentry just looked at him with a doubtful stare. Everyone in the garrison except the lady officer and Moha believed that Cirilo Ysmael is a guerilla corroborator. They were surprised when Moha "entrusted" their prisoner to this man. Pretending to be weak and sick, Fungway limped towards Cirilo as he asked for forgiveness. He said that he can hardly walk and feeling dizzy. In a very soft voice, Fungway said that he needed medical care. Fungway pretended to be collapsing as he was raising himself to stand. The lady officer called the guards and ordered them to deliver Fungway to Cirilo's house for proper medical care.

It was already beyond dusk when the "daughter" of Fungway was rescued. She was directly brought to him at Cirilo's house. It turned out that the said daughter is Cirilo's niece who they sent inside the cave to pretend as the captured daughter. She is now Anti

Paul Roderick. A. Ysmael

Ising Octaviano whose memory of the war is centered on this dramatic rescue attempt of her while she was alone in the cave with no captor. She was just brought there by a farmer and left her there just when the first shot was fired. Yes, she always recall the gunfire but she also will tell that there was no gunfight

Paul Roderick. A. Ysmael

Chapter Five: The Package

Deep in their camp inside the pine forest near the boundary of Abra and Ilocos Sur provinces, the members of the raiding team led by 2nd Lt. Carlitos Leiza and now, Anacleto Octaviano, were debating over their dinner of dried eel and sweet potato if the package is worth the life of Kiblongan and the liberty of Fungway. The camp which is commanded by Lt. Angel Moreno, welcomed them back. Composed of five huts, the camp is located on a dense forest jungle of native pine forest at the highest point of one of the hills of Northwestern Cordillera, about twenty kilometers from the town center. With the distance, they can afford to be noisy and be festive on their victorious raid. Everyone has an opinion as they sip some rice wine or "tapuy" that they got from a native farmer and placed them in their canteen. Leiza settled the debate by telling them that when they agreed to conduct the raid, the value of the package is immaterial. What is important is they got the package and pray that Marcial Esguerra will fulfill his word of giving them ammunition, fatigue uniform and food. He told his men that this is the reality of this war, although they have a common patriotic objective their unit has to fend for themselves. Their leader Angel Moreno nodded in approval. He told his men that what is important is to equip themselves with arms and ammo to survive the war, and get the needed recognition from the USAFIP-NL which they needed for possible integration with the armed forces. Of course, they also hope that eventually, they will have their

Paul Roderick. A. Ysmael

post war pensions as retired veterans of the United States. The bolomen then finished their meal in silence, thinking of various post war dreams as they just stared at the sealed package.

"To settle this issue, we will just open this thing," Carlitos broke the deafening silence, "We will know why Marcial Esguerra is offering us firearms and ammunition in exchange for this package as well as the possibility of joining his company."

He used his knife to break the sealed wooden box and the package revealed itself. They saw a map of Northern Luzon and documents written in Japanese characters. One looks like a memorandum dated December 24, 1943 with a place written as Kuala Lumpur, Malaysia that bears the signature of General Homa, the past commander of the Japanese Imperial Forces. Leiza observed that Japanese inscriptions were placed on the map for several towns. There signs and notations on the map bearing the names of the towns of Alaminos, Pangasinan, Tagudin, Ilocos Sur, Bessang Pass, Cervantes, Ilocos Sur and the towns of Bontoc, Mountain Province, the town of Kiangan, Ifugao all the way to the port town of Palanan, Isabela.

Carlitos looked closely at the map and he saw three sketches that looked like boxes with long arrows that seem to follow the major roads with Japanese characters as notations with characters that looked like dates. Still he was not able to discern from the said writings. He threw the package on the ground due to frustration "Bullshit! This is just their retreat map! The whole intelligence community and the guerilla fronts already know that the Japanese will be hiding in

Paul Roderick. A. Ysmael

the forests of Cordillera and will regroup as soon as they recover from their losses!"

"We just wasted the life of Kiblongan," seconded by Anacleto. The others cannot believe that they raided the garrison for information that everybody knows.

"Well, we just hope Benita can rescue Fungway!," Carlitos Leiza blurted, "that is, if her love for her country is stronger than her love for her Japanese boyfriend."

Moreno interrupted them and said "Children, what is important are the rifles and ammunition. The agreement is for one hundred pieces of rifles and pistols, I know Esguerra, and he has a reputation of standing by his word. Besides, those Japanese notations may mean more than their general plan of the Japanese retreat. Just re-seal it and give it to Esguerra then we wait for further orders."

Anacleto just nodded and joked, "I hope it pertains to something more than places and directions, I hope the map leads to a pot of gold." Anacleto slowly placed back the crumpled map inside the box. "Whatever it is worth, this is my first mission and I succeeded in entering a rat hole for this one, proving that in this war we cannot not simply say that size matters, every size has its own purpose."\

Every one laughed as they prepared to sleep beneath the watch of a couple of unarmed sentries.

The guerilla teams were awakened by the sentries early in the morning of the next day. Armed

Paul Roderick. A. Ysmael

men were approaching them carrying several arms cachet. The legendary Marcial Esguerra has arrived. True to his word, his men were carrying food supplies, Garand rifles, carbine sub-machine guns, uniforms and ammunition with one mortar as "bonus gift" for the whole the platoon. They handed over the package when Marcial Esguerra offered the team another job. They looked tired and sleepy, their faces reveal the wrath of the Battle of Bessang Pass which is still raging at that time. Around fifty men followed their leader, about ten have wounds uncovered by bandages and medical plasters. Two are limping but all seem to appear relieved and victorious.

Marcial Esguerra is short by military standards, standing below five feet and five inches, fairly built, with charismatic but stern eyes and his skin darken by the coastal towns of the Ilocos Region where he used to operate, usually receiving smuggled arms ammo and food supplies and carrying them into the jungles of the Cordillera and the Sierra Madre. His specialty is conducting surgical strikes and ambush attacks that made him one of the most decorated soldiers of Asia during the World War II. Later on however, his countrymen will doubt his medals. He fluently spoke the Ilocano dialect but his manners and diction reveal that he comes from the upper middleclass sector of Northern Luzon. He is known as an intelligent soldier whose main objective is to win his battle as all costs, risking his own life and limb in all his missions. Educated by the then world-admired public school system of the Americans, he entered the state university and joined the Advanced Reserve Officer's Training Course (UP ROTC). During the war,

Paul Roderick. A. Ysmael

the UP ROTC formed an armed guerilla contingent called the UP Hunters ROTC Battalion. The Hunters operated in the areas of Rizal and in the City of Manila. When Marcial Esguerra led an ambush near the boundary of Antipolo and Pasig in Rizal, he was not aware that several Makapilis were able to infiltrate his platoon. Instead of firing at the Japanese, some of his men captured him and turned him over to the platoon that they are about to ambush. Because of his reputation, he was held in Fort Santiago together with some American commanders. He escaped alone from the Fort, took a small watercraft and sailed towards Malabon. When he reached Pangasinan by land he, together with some relatives formed a guerilla command of around a hundred men, known to be the "E" Company. Theirs is the fifth company under the Battalion commended by then Colonel Narciso Ramos of Pangasinan. The "E" Company operated along the shoreline of Ilocos, conducting surgical strikes of rescuing captured Filipino and American officers, burning garrisons and sometime even churches used by the Japanese as offices. They also razed to the ground a couple of Ilocos towns who were friendly to the Japanese. When the USAFIP-NL massed along the towns of Tagudin and Sta. Cruz, Ilocos Sur in preparation to the epic battle of Bessang Pass, the "E" Company operated as a logistics and transport unit and rear blocking force, protecting the supply chain and the rear portion of the Allied Forces. The "E" Company's claim to fame is the annihilation of a combined Japanese and Filipino 'Makapili" Battalion which was sent to block the advance of the USAFIP-NL forces from Pangasinan to La Union in the Battle of Rosario, La Union. The "E" Company with precise

Paul Roderick. A. Ysmael

timing and effective strategy was able to trap the main part of the Japanese Battalion, including its artillery battery and machinegun trucks in a narrow trail in Kennon Road, blasted them with mines, shooting them both by precise sniper firing and immediate close-in attacks which sent the enemy into panic and disarray. This broke the main security force of the Japanese in Benguet and Northern Luzon. He only lost one man in that attack, whose memory is now celebrated by the 'Unknown Soldier" memorial at the junction of the National Hi-Way and the Poro Point Road. The Battle of Kennon Road paved the way for the "liberation" of the Summer Capital and the rest of Northern Luzon sending the Japanese to the Cordillera hinterlands and eventually to complete annihilation and surrender.

"I lost around half of my men for several reasons, one man was unfortunately killed by a Korean sniper in the La Union Japanese carnage, we thought we will have no casualty in that perfectly executed ambush, perhaps his time has come. Some died of malaria while travelling with me, some died at Bessang Pass and other opted to join the main guerilla front of Volckman under the command of Colonel Narciso Ramos," he said to Lt. Moreno. "I plan to enlist your team under my command, including the bolomen."

"Our main concern is our future after the war," Lt. Moreno lamented. Most of our bolomen are with us for the last three years. They are not regular fighters, we are not even sure if the Government will recognize our guerilla unit. We were organized by some officers

Paul Roderick. A. Ysmael

who survived the Death March from Bataan to Tarlac, but they left our group to join Volckman. We are considered a reconnaissance platoon, feeding them information beyond enemy lines."

"I am familiar with your personal skills. I already entrusted to you this important mission of recovering the package. You have been fighting on your own and I respect that. However, you can make yourself greater by joining us in our company. The war is not simply about your town, it is about the future of this nation as a whole. I can make you my reconnaissance platoon who will scout the enemy from striking distance, " Esguerra said, "I can also say that the success of this mission will answer all the doubts of your men about the future of this country, specifically out mission." Esguerra unintentionally emphasized "on their mission," yet the local guerilla commanders and their men still failed to notice it.

The platoon of Lt. Moreno and Carlitos Leiza had a meeting over dinner that day. Over the promise of including them in the regular army after the war, they agreed to enlist their forces under the command of Major Esguerra which was operating independently on a special mission. The heart and soul of the said mission is the package. The next day during formation, Major Esguerra, addressed the combined troops after the flag-raising ceremony.

"Gentlemen, good morning," the man in his thirty's spoke with authority, "Today, I will speak about the special mission which the Philippine High Command ordered us to accomplish."

Paul Roderick. A. Ysmael

Yamashita's Trucks of Treasures

"A year after the Japanese invasion, the Pacific High Command of the Allied Forces had information that the main target of the Japanese Imperial Army is to search, hoard and bring to the Japanese emperor's palace, the legendary treasures of the Sri Vijaya and the Madjapahit Empires that are scattered throughout Asia, from India to the Korean Peninsula. This explains why the imperial forces and their Asian conscripts kept on ransacking palaces, temples, Central Banks and Government fortresses of the various countries that they vanquished."

"They also attempted to loot the Chinese palaces but their treasures were not located due to British protection and most if not all are now owned by the English Monarchy."

"The hordes of gold and precious stones that they took from Thailand and Malaysia were reportedly landed in the port of Zamboanga in 1943 and were transferred to Fort Santiago the year later."

"I never believed this tale, until I was captured in Antipolo City and was locked at Fort Santiago. I saw a well-guarded area of the Fort. When I had an opportunity to escape after faking a heart attack, I decided to pass by the guarded dungeon as it was unlikely that I will use the area for my escape. I killed two guards and in the process of hiding, I personally saw the hoards of gold, stones and Buddha statues. I was able to get this bracelet of a sultan as proof of the existence of the treasure."

Esguerra held high a golden bracelet with Arabic inscription for everyone to see.

Paul Roderick. A. Ysmael

"I reported back to the USAFIP-NL and told them this discovery but everyone thought I was just hallucinating due to hunger, and this gold bracelet may have been sold to me by a Muslim Sultan from Mindanao."

"But my friends in the ROTC Hunters believed my tale and they reported it to the Philippine High Command who commissioned our company for this mission."

"From then on, searching for this treasure became my passion. I personally believe that if we recover this cache of gold and precious stones, we will be able to liberate ourselves from the chains of poverty that was caused both by colonization of our foreign masters and greed of the few of our countrymen. The Philippine High Command knows how dedicated I am in this search. I diligently followed its trail until I found out that the escape route is also the treasures trail. I promise you that not a single piece of any jewelry will benefit me, we shall turn over this treasure to our National Treasury."

"When General Douglas Mac Arthur landed in the Gulf of Leyte, the Japanese panicked and decided to evacuate their treasure northward."

"General Romulo called me to report in Cebu and I was tasked to monitor the treasure and possibly recover it for the country. This is what the mission is all about, this is the real package!"

Paul Roderick. A. Ysmael

The guerillas were stunned by the revelation. Even Esguerra's own men never knew about what the real mission is all about.

Paul Roderick. A. Ysmael

Part Six: The Golden Trail

Now known as the "Mountain Trail," Halsema Highway stretches from La Trinidad Benguet to Bontoc Mountain Province. It has terrestrial tributaries, the Tagudin-Cervantes-Mankayan Road or the Bessang Pass Trial and the Cervantes-Bontoc Road. Constructed parallel and occasionally crossing tributaries of the rampaging Abra (Amburayan) River and passing several mountain settlements, mines, ranches and vegetable farms, the mountain trail is the main road artery of the Cordilleras. Built by logging

Paul Roderick. A. Ysmael

and mining companies with help from the Spanish ranch and hacienda owners in the during the 18th Century, the trail was further developed by the Americans as an alternate route to Baguio from the Ilocos Region. It is the main route of merchants from both areas trading to each other. If you add all its tributaries, the mountain trail is about 250 kilometers long of winding and treacherous roads, sandwiched by ravines, steeply sloped mountains and thick pin forests. It has at least two tunnels and several narrow bridges. Around ten kilometers from the coastal highway at Tagudin, Ilocos Sur, the mountain trail abruptly elevates to about 50 feet above sea level and continuously ascends until it reaches its maximum elevation of around 900 feet at Bessang Pass. It slowly descends to the Cervantes Town proper. It will again ascend until it reaches Halsema Highway's Highest Point which is around 6,000 feet above sea level and ends at the boundary of La Trinidad and Atok, Benguet. As the highway traverses its course, you will also see the diversity of the communities as you pass by. Near the lowlands are patches of huts and houses occupied by the simple and industrious Ilocano families, where nearly every house has at least a "carabao" or water buffalo, the Philippine beast of burden.The carabaos are tied at the yard of their masters, ready to till the nearby farm any day before the heat of noon and after three in the afternoon. Around the houses are vegetables for the daily sustenance of its planters. There also a number of chicken, swine and goats which are destined for family occasion and town fiestas. The Ilocanos are known for their simplicity and prudence. Their daily food is largely vegetarian. Hence, they have dishes which are

Paul Roderick. A. Ysmael

entirely meatless. They even feed on exotic grass and leaves with little or no cooking at all. Their culture and food are the secret of their longevity and strength. They claim to have the culture of prudent spending bordering to stingy because of the topography of the region. The coastal towns actually have semi-arid lands that only a dedicated and hardworking farmer can transform it into an agricultural farm. They only have meat on special occasions and for the more affluent, every Sunday lunch. This explains why each and every Ilocano home looks like a garden of vegetables and surrounded by their favorite "saluyot" herb, which is their favorite dish. As the highway ascends into the mountains, you will see several Igorot communities of various tribes. These highland communities will give you a refreshing view of vegetable terraces surrounding a community of log cabins and native huts. The ethnic male population are clad in colorful G-strings or "bahag' and the women are wear similarly radiant and exotically adorned native dresses. They are generally friendly and they welcome every stranger with smiling stares. The Cordillera natives are generally shorter, wide bodied and with larger legs due. Their built is due to their frequent climbs and descends at their mountainous settlements. They are largely dependent on "camote" or sweet potato tubers and mountain rice. Men wear hairs with a traditional haircut that make their heads look like coconut husks. They may have common features but they belong to several tribes. For the expert in Cordillera ethnology, he can identify the said tribes by looking at the color combination of their clothing. With predominantly flamingo red color, the g-strings and native dresses have bright yellow, ivory

Paul Roderick. A. Ysmael

white and other bright colors. Social status is determined by the head gears of men and tattoos on women. The Gran Cordillera Region then was deceptively peaceful cradled by blue mountain peaks if viewed from afar. At its bosom are happy communities. But these communities are being disturbed both by war that ravaged its natural beauty and by the cultural intrusions both by the native lowlanders and foreigners. It will soon be home not only to its native people but also to Japanese stragglers, American miners and Ilocano migrants all seeking for the treasure that the mountain range holds.

Aside from being witness to the rampaging jungle war that led to the capture of the Japanese Commander of Asia, General Tomoyuki Yamashita, the mountain trail is also a theatre of the hunt for the Trucks of Gold.

The message of Marcial Esguerra greatly contributed to the overall silence of the guerilla camp. Lt. Moreno sent around seven of his men to conduct perimeter patrol at a distance of about one kilometer around the camp. Perimeter patrols are usually conducted by shifts. Sometimes the patrol doubles as hunters, bringing home wild ducks, wild boars and in some occasions, the rare Cordillera mouse deer. Standing around two feet in height, the Cordillera male mouse deer has a beautiful crown of branching horns, with white spots, to distinguish it from the bigger Philippine Deer. Its meat is tender and tasty but its speed and extra-ordinary sense of smell make it the most difficult beast to hunt in this side of the world.

Paul Roderick. A. Ysmael

The perimeter foot patrol is conducted to avoid detection by the Makapilis and to prevent Japanese stragglers from inflicting harm against any of his encamped men. The Makapilis usually report to the Cervantes garrison their sighting of guerilla camps and Moha has the habit of always attacking in full force complete with an artillery complement. For several occasions, the foot patrol was forced to execute a whole platoon of Makapilis in order to prevent them from reporting. The frequent scouting of the Makapilis also explains why the guerillas were forced to camp around ten kilometers from the town proper. They were initially camped near a sugar plantation several meters away from the town hall until the Makapilis torched their camp and were nearly annihilated by the swarming Japanese.

Aside from the foot patrol, security is also ensured by the bolomen who are stationed just outside the camp's gate and serve as sentry guards. Several guerillas are also stationed dispersed around the camp's premises but those who have the most recent mission are usually allowed to rest.

Inside the main camp, the "E" Company is starting to re-organize itself into several platoons of forty men each. The original platoon has been split into two to integrate the bolomen. The main platoon is commanded by Maj. Marcial Esguerrra's Ex-Officer, Capt. Fabian Ver and the rear platoon is commanded by a certain Capt. Mario de los Reyes of Vigan, Ilocos Sur. The advance and reconnaissance platoon is commanded by Lt. Angel Moreno with the first platoon commanded by 2Lt. Carlitos Leiza. The first platoon

Paul Roderick. A. Ysmael

has been divided into two special units of seven men each that will act as their scout.

In the evening of that day, the platoon commanders and squad leaders were met by Esguerra and briefed them about the map. It turned out that the map is the escape rout of the Japanese treasure loot. Esguerra introduced his interpreter, Danilo Sato, a Japanese sired Ilocano and janitor of the Japanese Embassy to explain the details of the map.

"This map illustrates the direction where the trucks are going. The three boxes at the bottom symbolizes three trucks," Sato pointed at the three boxes at the lower right side of the map, "the Japanese characters speaks of stops and drop-off. This means that the trucks are allowed to refuel, their crew to rest and to drop some of the things"

Sato then pointed to the Japanese characters marking several town centers.

"It means that from Lingayen to Bessang Pass, the trucks can only rest for thirty minutes in each stop in Alaminos, Pangasinan and Tagudin, Ilocos Sur. The journey of the trucks started last year and we believed that they are now parked near the Japanese caves near the Bessang Pass waiting for further instructions. This explains why the main Japanese forces are still in Bessang Pass."

"The Lingayen to Tagudin trip occurred in November 5 or 6, 1944, about the same date when we engaged their blocking force at the Battle of Camp One in Kennon Road. It appears that they were planning to

Paul Roderick. A. Ysmael

travel via Kenner Road towards Baguio but when we intercepted their forces there, they went straight north. Unfortunately, we considered it as a minor troop movement," Marcial Esguerra interrupted.

"It was our impression that the treasure should be well-guarded. Our scouts reported that the convoy is only composed of three trucks and five jeeps with light arms. They were travelling fast and at that time, there are still no available force that can engage them as the guerillas were still re-grouping near the Pangasinan-Tarlac border and negotiation with the Hukbalahap Movement (communist anti-Japanese force) for possible integration was still ongoing."

"Your forces here were still mere bands of men with no sufficient guns and bullets. For that size of enemy force, we needed the same size of men and arms, which we used at the Kennon Road Battle."

"Aside from that, "Sato continued, "we were suspicious of Volkmann and his American officers, our Philippine High Command was clear and specific that the Americans should not know anything about this one."

"As the Japanese are nearing their main command force, they became conscious on the security of their treasure. Their forces in Suyo Ilocos Sur, as indicated by this Japanese notation met up with the convoy."

"We tried to intercept them here in Barrio Butac," Esguerra pointed at the map, " just before the

Paul Roderick. A. Ysmael

ascent to the Bessang Pass but we were too early and our troops were detected. We had to retreat and flee towards Volkmann's headquarters, we were really after this map and the trucks."

"After several attempts, we decided to get the escape map first. We conducted a clandestine attack against Yamashita's bunker, several meters away from Bessang Pass (now known as the Yamashita Cave). We did not find this package to confirm the existence of the treasure and to have the map, but after torturing a Korean guard, we got a word that the documents are at the Cervantes Garrison. When w met Volkmann, we learned about the friendship between Fungway and Moha. So, we decided to contact you."

The group continued their analysis over the blueprint of the Golden Trail.

Paul Roderick. A. Ysmael

Chapter Seven: Escape from the Empire's Wrath

Two weeks have passed since Cirilo was appointed as the "guardian" of Fungway. Like a father, Cirilo nursed Fungway back to his health, feeding him of the traditional "apro ti igat" or eel's bile and "tinola" or chicken soup. In less than five days from his release from the garrison, Fungway already regained his strength. To avoid suspicion, however, Fungway just lied low and avoided any contact with the guerillas. He just helped in the daily chores at Cirilo's rice mill, carrying sacks after sacks of palay into the mill's bin and packing them into cavans of milled rice.

Paul Roderick. A. Ysmael

Sometimes he tends the sari-sari store, fetches the carabaos and cooked supper. Occasionally, the Japanese guards checked him. The Makapilis who were already watching Cirilo's house on a daily basis for the last three years, doubled their searching eyes every hour, minute and second. The problem however is that they use their eyes too much to the extent of forgetting their other senses. Seeing nothing, they strained their eyes more and they failed to use their ears in order to hear the whispers in the house. They did not also utilize their sixth sense so they did not feel the emotions inside it. As they tired their eyes watching Fungway was doing his daily works, they recklessly ignored the whispering which became louder and louder as the raging emotion to revolt intensified inside the house. Unknown to their suspicious eyes, Fungway already heard the whispered instructions as to how he and Cirilo's family will be rescued before the Americans will reach the town.

    Two weeks after the raid of the garrison, summer has arrived with the month of March. The cold winds from the northern hills and the mist of the Cordillera are now being warmed by the hot southern breeze and the humid air from the West Philippine Sea that lies west of the Cordillera range. The Tamaang Valley has now turned from golden yellow to dry brown. The ripe rice stalks are already harvested and the leaves are left to dry down. It is a practice of the farmers to just leave the grass dry in order for them to fertilize the land once more and ready it for planting once the rains drench the fields in the month of June.

Paul Roderick. A. Ysmael

The raid and burning of the armory and the capture of Fungway is a folk tale no more. Everyone is now back to his or her daily chores. To the people, Fungway, is now just "one of the workers of Manong Ilong" as Cirilo was fondly called.

Amidst the raging battle in the hills surrounding Bessang Pass, the farmers were able to harvest their rice on time. They just looked up in the hills once in a while as to rest their tired bodies and view the trajectory of mortars from the guerillas and the Japanese that exchange at the dark horizon. The sight of flying fireballs from both of the warring sides gave them light during the night when the moon was covered by the dark fog and when the full moon did not appear twice in the month. The booming sounds of the guns and the rattling of rifles gave them a musical background as they rushed to end the harvest season and fill their landlords' barns in time for the Holy Week celebrations. Unmindful of the raging battle 20 kilometers away, the farmers busied themselves at their fields, cutting the rice stalks and threshing out the grains. Slowly the golden rice stalks were taken away and replaced by the brick dry, chocolate brown empty field. The land would rest for a while and so with the toiling hands. Their beasts of burden are given the much needed furlough. Like the farmers, they are given a month to just relax at the nearest mud pond. Every man and his animal will have adequate rest until the next planting season. The battle is raging but their lives must go on. They eat, pray, love and rest for a while. They believe that their lives depended more on the hands of their landlords rather than on the result of the World War.

Paul Roderick. A. Ysmael

The month of March was relatively peaceful and quite. The guerillas in observance of the Holy Week ceased in their harassment attacks. The Japanese and their Korean conscripts were seen buying sacks of rice (at that time a sack of rice is worth a sack of "Japanese Money" which were issued in lieu of the Philippine Peso) instead of doing their routine drills and patrols. They are filling up their granary. They were preparing the food supplies for the "rainy days."

The church was filled with people for the whole week as the processions and the Holy Week devotions were observed. From Palm Sunday to Easter Sunday, the town's center of solemn commemorative celebration was the Church. Palm Sunday is celebrated by the blessing of coconut and palm leaves which come in various artistic designs. They are either shaped like birds, fruits and insects. Monday was the choir competition where Lenten Songs are sang during the evening by competing choirs. The prize is not much of money but the absolution of the sins of those who have the best performance. Tuesday is the dramatization of the Christian Crusade in the Holy Land better known as the "comedia." Cirilo Ysmael is known as the writer and director of this traditional show. The comedia is about the battle of the Spanish Catholics and the invading Moors, including the romance that blossomed between the Islamic princes and Catholic princesses. It is therefore a love story of the warring royalties who sacrificed their unending loves to each other in favor of their Faith. Being such, the show was consistently highly attended even if the story is consistently repeated every year. Usually the town's mestizos and meztizas, or children of the

Paul Roderick. A. Ysmael

landlords play the lead roles and the children of the farmers play as their aides, consorts and girl Fridays. There is always a comedic pair or comedic pairs, giving some funny breaks to the passionate drama that the story conveys. The show is actually the subtle affirmation of the social strata of its time which is the real show in this side of earth. Just like its script which Cirilo used every year, the enthusiasm of the people never changed. The folks always troop to watch the show annually. Their main motivation is not the story but to know who among them is playing the role of the protagonists for that year.

Holy Wednesday is devoted for prayers and singing of the "pasyon." It is the singing in monotonic rhyme of the passion of Christ from his arrival in Jerusalem to his eventual crucifixion in the washed hands of Pontius Pilate and the ranting Jews. This will be followed by the Celebration of the Last Supper at Holy Thursday, the commemoration of the Crucifixion of Jesus on Good Friday, then by the Celebration of the Holy Spirit and Renewal of Baptismal Vows of a Catholic on Black Saturday. The Philippine Holy Week ends gloriously on Easter Sunday, where the triumph of Jesus over death is celebrated through his Resurrection.

So, the Lenten season on that year was a divine opportunity for everyone. For the townsfolk, it was a time to cleanse their souls, for the invading the Japanese it was time to reinforce their barracks and pile up their supplies for a possible "last stand" in the Cordilleras. For the guerillas, it was time for intelligence work and a reprieve from the repeated

Paul Roderick. A. Ysmael

failures to conquer the Bessang Pass. During this Holy Week in Cervantes, all the wounds both of the sinful souls and weary bodies were treated by the healing rituals of religion and festive celebrations.

That period of two weeks was more than enough for Fungway to plan his return to the battle front. Cirilo on the other hand was trying to evade detection by utilizing the Lenten serenity of the town and his active involvement in the religious celebrations. Despite his efforts, however, the Makapilis were slowly unmasking the real allegiance of Cirilo Ysmael, whom the Japanese appointed as the guardian of their prisoner called Fungway!

In the evening of Black Saturday, 2nd Lt. Carlitos Leiza's sent one of his men to get some canned goods and other supplies from his Uncle Cirilo. The guerillas were also preparing for their upcoming mission, and food is part of the said preparation. Disguised as a coffee trader from Bontoc, the guerilla delivered a sack to Cirilo pretending to exchange the same for sardines and corned beef through barter. The guerrilla's disguise of an Igorot haircut and old g-string passed the searching eyes of the Makapilis who were spying on Cirilo. They did not bother to search or question the said front man. What gave away the disguise was when, about two weeks later, the sack which was supposed to be containing coffee beans was seen by a Makapili in a trash can containing guava leaves. It still appeared unopened but it is now left inside the trash can. This raised the level of the Makapilis suspicion as they inspected the pile of garbage. One of the Makapilis went to Cirilo's "sari-sari" store and

Paul Roderick. A. Ysmael

pretended to buy coffee beans. He told the store helper that he wanted the freshest delivery or newest beans at the price that is better than the market. Sensing an interrogation, the store helper said that he will ask the store owner which sack was the newest among the stockpile. The Makapili said that he prefers the one delivered last Black Saturday. Feigning ignorance, the helper claimed not to have known any delivery on the Black Saturday. "It may have been directly sold to Manong Ilong," he said. "I was not the one who accepted it, so I cannot tell which the is newest stock."

The probing did not end there. The Makapilis went around the store to verify if there was really coffee delivery in exchange for the canned goods. They were convinced that there was no barter. It was plain donation to the revolutionary cause of what they call bandits, masquerading as guerilla front. Their canine sense enabled them to trace the footprints of the guerilla logistics man. They noticed that the footprints led to the northern trails which was northward to Abra the guerilla front's lair, instead of returning to the east. If the man was really a coffee trader, he cold have traveled back towards the Mountain Province, where the best coffee is grown in the islands. Because they knew in their hearts that the Japanese commander will have a hard time believing them, the Makapilis did not report immediately their discovery. The had to gather additional proof of treason committed by Cirilo against the Empire of the Sun, otherwise their report might be used against them. They wanted to dig deeper into the northern woodlands in order to unravel the secret liaisons between Cirilo Ysmael and his guerilla relatives. The Makapilis however hesitated to

Paul Roderick. A. Ysmael

go northward when they realized that their fighting and scouting skills are no match to the notorious killing instincts of "Itos" Leiza and his men. So they just decided to pile up their evidence further from the activities of Cirilo and his household. They are sure, they were be able to lay their case against Cirilo in proper time.

The Makapilis' wait for proper time was racing against Cirilo's plan of finally leaving the town and join the guerilla camp as civilian community leader. He was informed that with the growing strength of the guerillas, came the improvement of their firepower. As they became a potent defensive force, civilians started to live near the camp. The guerillas gained confidence to the point that some already brought with them their families in order to escape the heightened abuses of the Makapilis. The problem with an old town is that nearly everybody is an acquaintance of everyone. The Makapilis knew which of the families in town has a guerilla son, father, cousin or in-law. The Makapilis used the abusive tactic of getting the mothers or fathers as prisoners in order to force the guerilla to surrender. The treason committed by a family member is a crime of the whole family. When parents offered their freedom and lives for the revolutionary cause, the Makapilis went further. They did not only torture the fathers, mothers and siblings. They began raping wives, sisters and mothers of the guerillas. This barbaric act naturally called for severe retaliations from the guerilla front. Makapilis were ambushed and arrested and hanged by the guerillas in the pine trees. Some also raped the wives and daughters of the Makapilis. The eye already demanded for the eye, and

Paul Roderick. A. Ysmael

the tooth was hammered down by steel-like retaliation of assassination and murder. Houses were torched and animals butchered for the celebration of the victor. Starting as a war of invasion, the Makapilis transformed it into a civil war. Innocent civilians became refugees, slowly the town's harvest is being transferred to the hills as more and more families contributed a man or a woman in the guerilla's revolutionary cause.

Cirilo Ysmael is a father of six ladies, a teenage lad and a little boy. As the civil war in the town raged, he planned to lead his family and servants into a safe haven. When he learned of the interrogation of his storekeeper, he realized it was time to commence his evacuation plan. The following morning, he emptied one of his barns and transferred its contents to a nearby farm that was owned by a friend. He volunteered to host the Easter Dinner at the garrison with the camp commander as his guest and Fungway as the celebrator, thanking the Emperor for his life. As they broke bread and shared rice with the empire's main military man, Cirilo's servants were busy clandestinely evacuating the valuables and rice of their master. The Makapilis in their eagerness to nail down Cirilo stayed to observe him in the garrison, giving all the opportunity to the servants to execute their master's instructions.

By the end of March and when April heat started to dry the swamps and creeks, emptying the waters of the ponds and springs, Cirilo has already emptied all his barns. In fact he has already built his hut inside the guerilla camp.

Paul Roderick. A. Ysmael

Then sometime in May, during the great inferno raid done by the guerillas with the mission of weakening the supply chain of the Japanese and Makapilis for the Battle of Bessang Pass, Cirilo and his family together with Fungway, evacuated to the guerilla camp while the whole town was razed by the torching of the guerillas. Even Cirilo's old ancestral home was not spared including his near-empty store and rice milling machine. The raging fire became their shelter from the eyes of the Makapilis as they hurriedly proceeded north to the guerilla camp with the help of Leiza's men and Fungway. There, Cirilo became the trusted caretaker of the guerillas ammo and food depot until the end of the war.

The guerillas only spared the Church, where the family of the Makapilis hid. The Makapilis know that the religious faith of the Catholic guerillas will temper their revolutionary wrath and the Church will be the safest place to hide their families. Indeed, all the women, children and the old who took the old church as their refuge were left unharmed. In fact, the guerillas even gave them food and medicine before they left. That inferno raid was instrumental in weakening the logistical support of the Japanese forces in Bessang Pass. The Japanese granary was torched, the Makapili detachment too was charred into oblivion. Twenty of the one hundred guerilla men perished so with fifty bolomen but their lives were not wasted as they broke the back of the Cordillera supply chain of the Japanese. By that time the Japanese garrison was supplying rice and meat to their camps in Bessang Pass and in their hideouts in the Mountain Provinces.

Paul Roderick. A. Ysmael

Chapter Eight: Guardians of the Treasures

Toki and Tomo were able to get the trust and confidence of Moha due to their gallantry in the February 15, 1945 raid of the Japanese Imperial Army-Cervantes Garrison. These two young men were not even supposed to be sentries that night. They just volunteered to assume the posts of their subordinates who were drunk. Since then, Moha eyed them for more important missions and took them out from their MP duties. The Japanese commander assigned them back to the regular infantry in order to make good use of their talents, dedication and bravery. So when General Yamashita gave this important mission of transporting and securing the trucks of treasures to him, Moha already knew whom will he entrust its fulfillment. He knew very well that these two young men could very well help him in making the mission successful. He needs young and trustworthy men, with above-average skills and intelligence. These two young men exactly possess these traits.

On June 01, 1945, Moha was directed to report to the "Yamashita Cave," a medium sized-natural cave complex somewhere near the Bessang Pass. He was called to receive a Mission Order from the highest ranking Japanese Officer in the Philippines, General Yamashita. The Japanese general was then comfortably holed up in his mountainous fortress courtesy of the steep and sharp ridges of the Western Cordilleras. The height of the mountain ridge is so perfect for military purposes, in a clear day you can

Paul Roderick. A. Ysmael

see the West Philippine Sea or South China Sea miles below. If one is equipped with telescope, he can even see what are inside the sailing vessels. While the direct distance from the shore is less than fifty kilometers, the winding trail with steep climb makes it difficult to access. The location is so strategic to be a vantage point because you can see even a crawling salamander a kilometer below from above, except if the portion of the mountain is covered by the thick morning fog or the thick sayote vegetation. Yamashita's forces can clearly see any attacking force from below. Aerial attack is also difficult as the irregular height of the mountain range makes every plane an easy target of anti-aircraft guns while the thick vegetation of the pass restricts the view of even a seasoned airborne gunner or bomber. This is the place where Yamashita temporarily hid the three trucks of treasures. However, the Emperor did not wish to hide the treasures there forever. He wanted them to be transported to Japan! This was an order and Yamashita has patiently planned how to execute it. It will be very obvious if he will take the treasures with him in his retreat. He should part with the treasures and send it through a separate convoy. After consulting his generals and field commanders, they had a consensus that the appropriate person to do the job should be the one who is familiar with the Cordillera Mountains. Among the field commanders only Makoto Moha has the extensive knowledge of the Cordillera terrain as he commanded their advance forces that are now stationed in Cervantes and operating as far as Bontoc and Banawe, Ifugao. Moha knows the terrain too well that he can tell which mountain is easier to climb and where the guerillas are encamped. Moha has been responsible in raids of guerilla camps behind their lines and the reason why the Japanese in Bessang Pass have not been attacked from behind is due to the relentless operations of Moha. So while his main forces took care of their frontlines, Moha secured their rear. The main advantage of their positions is actually the terrain that favors anyone who controls Bessang Pass. The only risk of the fortress is an attack that comes from behind them. However, with Moha at their back, it may never happen.

After several battles and fierce attempts, the American and Filipino forces failed to just even climb the first hill towards Bessang Pass in Butac, Suyo, Ilocos Sur. The steep hill was protected by the Japanese artillery batteries that had clear uninterrupted view of their ascending enemies. In fact, the USAFIP-NL has planned a major attack to take-over the pass in December 1944, using the thick fog and lush "sayote vegetation" as cover. Unfortunately, the northern winds came only in late January that year, delaying the fog and giving the Japanese a clear view of the naked trail. The Japanese were able to cut the advancing forces by mining the Butac Bridge. This gave the attacking forces their worst setback in the eight-month battle of Bessang Pass.

Details of the attack, as recounted by aging veterans, says that a Battalion sized USAFIP-NL and guerilla joint forces attempted their first ascent to the Pass in December 30, 1945. This was in time for the cold months where the area's visibility is restricted both by fog and occasional rainfall. It is also the time where the grassy vegetation is at its thickest and

Paul Roderick. A. Ysmael

where sayote and camote (sweet potato) vines provide the needed cover. They massed below the first hill at around 0300 HRS taking advantage of the shadow of the Cordillera range. Fully camouflaged and armed mostly with assault automatic weapons, they massed upwards towards the first Japanese artillery battery, twenty kilometers below the main pass. Unfortunately, the Japanese sensed their planned attack and the Japanese transformed their supposed surprise attack into a big setback.

Two Igorot Makapilis at that time were on their way to the Japanese advance post from Suyo. The Makapilis were sent to get supplies from the Suyo town market. They incidentally saw the advancing forces on their way. In fact, they were even accosted by some bolomen but managed to get their way out by pretending to be traders, selling canned goods to the ethnic Igorots in the uptown barrios of Suyo. The Makapilis immediately reported what they saw to the Japanese advance post commander who dispatched a team of explosive experts towards the Butac Bridge. The said bridge is the only infrastructure link between Suyo and Cervantes towns, which is separated by the Sudipen River or the River Bio. After allowing three of the five military trucks inside the long-spanned bridge, the Japanese explosive team detonated their mines, instantly killing around fifty Americans and Filipinos, badly wounding hundreds of them. Around a hundred of the wounded were eventually finished off by machine-gun and artillery fire. It was a massacre at the foot of the Bessang Pass and the first major sacrifice of human lives on the side of the allied forces.

Paul Roderick. A. Ysmael

Since then, the American and Filipino forces busied themselves regrouping and recruiting more men while planning how to take the "pass" from the Japanese. They limited themselves into surgical attacks to Japanese positions and foxholes, sometimes neutralizing machine gun pods, recovering small artillery and ammunition. They satisfied themselves harassing the enemy by protracted attack for lack of a strategy to engage in a conventional warfare. When the Cervantes Garrison was successfully attacked, Volkmann's hopes were resuscitated. In fact the December massacre of the USAFIP forces was a result of his over-eagerness to engage the Japanese in a conventional war. Ignoring and deliberately against the contrary view of the Filipino guerilla commanders who were familiar with the terrain, Volkmann insisted on massing up and overwhelming the advance command post of the Japanese who were fully armed and well-entrenched. The December 30, 1944 carnage will always be remembered by those who survived as a perfect portrait of underestimating a clearly well-entrenched and advantageously positioned enemy's capability due to unreasonable haste. From then on, Volkmann became more careful in executing his attacks. He learned to rely on the local commanders' knowledge of the terrain and natural obstacles. Before the end of May 1945, new troops from the United States Seventh Fleet and Sixth Army arrived in Ilocos. They brought with them new rifles and machine guns, communication equipment and artillery. A cavalry battalion was also sent to improve their mobility. This was complemented by the freed troops in Bataan. With new recruits from La Union, Volkmann re-organized his guerilla units into infantry, cavalry and light

Paul Roderick. A. Ysmael

artillery. By that time, Volkmann gave in to Esguerra's request for more "command autonomy" as long as he coordinated his troop movement with the main guerilla front in order to avoid friendly armed encounters. In fact, Esguerra was not also receiving any order from the Philippine authorities as to how he will conduct his operations. He was on his own. These are the reasons why Esguerra's forces were reluctantly recognized as a guerilla contingent by the Filipino and American authorities. Yet, they were accorded some degree of both respect and resistance. Volkmann later on discovered that more than capturing Yamashita, Esguerra's obsession was to get the treasures of the Emperor, which he himself doubted its existence. The American commander regarded Esguerra more of a treasure hunter than a Filipino soldier. To his credit, Esguera was honest and open in his priorities. He recruited his own men, financed them from their family's modest wealth and was able to feed them with the support of his friends. The politicians were also supportive of his efforts, especially in his attacks against the Japanese positions. Esguerra has already gained popularity among the local populace because of his legendary exploits. His reputation precedes his presence in every town. His name became a legend. The news of his victories made him a folk hero and most young men wanted to join his forces either as regular fighter, boloman or simple runner. They just wanted to be identified with Esguerra by whatever kind of association. After the war, nearly all of the older men have stories about Esguerra, and every man was claiming credit from each of Esguerra's medals. As every Filipino of his generation remembers, he was the most decorated Asian soldier of World War II. Few

Paul Roderick. A. Ysmael

however will remember that his fierce hunt against the Japanese aggressors was impelled mainly by these trucks of treasures. Despite his increasing endearment to the masses and his gain of respect from civilians and combatants alike, Esguerra's superiors in the Philippine military and the US High command never believed his story about the trucks of treasures. They were just exploiting him as he was effective in hunting down Japanese contingents. While Esguerra has questionable obedience to his superiors, they knew that his loyalty to the country is unparalleled by any soldier in that war.

Both sides knew that the great battle will be fought before the rainy days as the Americans will prefer to attack during the dry summer months. By the first day of June, the Americans and their Filipino counterparts have already controlled all major towns of Ilocos, including the commercial town of Candon and San Fernando, La Union. They were also able to isolate the Bessang Pass forces and had reports that Japanese ammo is already short. The surgical strikes and occasional harassment worked to their favor. As they kept on attacking the Japanese, they were fired upon by artillery and mortar fire, slowly reducing the logistics of the enemy. On the other hand, for facing the last concentration of Japanese forces, supply from Manila and other cities were being concentrated to Volkmann's forces. The Filipino commanders knew this is the proper time to launch an attack. The Filipino officers also welcomed the decision of Gen. Douglas Mac Arthur to retain Volkmann and his officers to lead the allied armies in Bessang Pass. They knew that Volkmann, despite his differences with

Paul Roderick. A. Ysmael

Esguerra and even with Moreno and Leiza, earned his right to lead the attack on Bessang Pass. Volkmann was the only American commander who defied Mac Arthur's order to surrender. From Bataan, he managed to go northward with a handful of American soldiers and stayed in Abra. He was able to evade arrest. In one surgical strike that he commanded after his escape, he was hit twice by Japanese bullet in the back. He hid in Bontoc while recuperating from his wounds but one of the bullets still resides in his spine and became his lifelong souvenir from Bessang Pass. When Volkmann recovered from the near fatal shots, he went around Luzon, searching for American and Filipino soldiers who escaped the Death March. He organized them, recruited former communist insurgents and young civilians until he was able to complete one army division. After three long years of building his forces while waiting for the liberation by the Americans, he maintained a strong guerilla force in Northern Luzon. Volkmann called his forces the United States Armed Forces in the Philippines-North Luzon or the famed USAFIP-NL.

General Yamashita was already aware of their situation as a losing army at that time. After the Fall of Manila, followed by the landing by General Mac Arthur at the Lingayen Gulf and the Fall of Baguio City all in the hands of the returning Americans, he knew that his hold on the pass is already jeopardized. He is now isolated in the mountains and surviving only with some clandestine delivery of ammo and supplies coming from their supporters in the lowlands. Even the number of their secret sympathizers, however, is now dwindling due to the increased intelligence and

Paul Roderick. A. Ysmael

surveillance work by the Philippine Military. Sensing danger, he summoned his field commanders in preparation for his retreat.

With his five remaining divisions scattered all over the Cordilleras, Yamashita decided to concentrate his men in Bessang Pass as he planned an eventual escape from the Philippines. A true Japanese Samurai warrior, Yamashita was ready to give up his life through their traditional "harakiri" in case he fails in his mission. His enemies will soon know that his escape plan is not about him leaving the Philippines. On the contrary, the success of the escape plan has nothing to do with his life or capture. In fact, he wanted himself to be visible and captured so that his mission would be a success.

Col. Moha, who successfully defended the Cervantes Garrison from the Philippine guerilla forces, was called to report to the Bessang Pass camp for an important mission. Moha was instructed to leave the garrison and proceed to the famed Banaue Rice Terraces through the Mountain Trail. He was instructed to use the Halsema Highway and reach Banaue through the Bontoc-Benguet Road. He was supposed to command around five hundred Japanese soldiers and Korean conscripts and several hundreds of Makapilis, a light armor phalanx and three big trucks. Yamashita told him to guard the three trucks with their lives and if any force comes near, it should be repulsed at all costs. He said that most of the empire's objective in the war are inside the three trucks. Indeed, the legend of the trucks of treasures and gold is true and Moha will be their guardian from this day on. In case they are unable to defend the said trucks, they should either bury them or crash them in the deepest ravines of Halsema Highway. If they succeed, they should bring the trucks to Palanan, Isabela and they will be fetched by a submarine. The trucks contain the most precious treasures artifacts of the Sri Vijaya and the Majapahit Empires. These two empires were known in ancient history to have successfully identified and mined the treasures and precious stones of South and Southeast Asia. They manufactured ancient treasures jewelries that reached even the Pharaohs of Egypt and even used by the conquerors from Greece and Rome. When these ancient Asian empires were conquered or driven away to oblivion by the Europeans, they hid their treasures in several temples. The Japanese also got treasures from Buddhist temples of Thailand and its neighboring countries. Among the listed artifacts are various golden masks and golden statues, used for burial and as deity, respectively, by the ancient empires, three different sizes of golden Buddha statues from Thailand, although these are hollow and made of near pure treasures, inside them are precious stones. The Japanese also hoarded other artifacts which the Sri Vijaya emperors used both as sacred ornaments and jewelry containers. They were hidden by the monks, Malaysian sultans and Bornean rajahs, in various temples. There was also the golden statue of the Komodo Dragon, which was worshipped by ethnic Polynesians who once inhabited the island of Java and Sumatra in Indonesia. According to Yamashita's records, the Golden Komodo measured five long feet, made of pure gold. When the Sri Vijaya emperor captured it from the natives, he decorated the golden

Paul Roderick. A. Ysmael

komodo with two 5 karat diamonds believed to be shipped from Africa to form two circular eyes and studded their surroundings with emerald chips. Ruby, sapphire, amethyst, onyx and other precious stones were also used to decorate the dragon's body. The ancient emperor also placed nails over its hands and feet made of black diamonds. The collection of the golden royal masks dated back to 1000 BC. This means that these masks covered the faces of different ancient ethnic kings and queens even before the ancient empires were established. These masks were dug by Thai and Indian archeologists in search for the ancient Asian man near the plains of their major riverside settlements. The trucks also carried gold laced boxes where jewelry ranging from bracelets to nose-rings, ear-rings, royalty rings and necklace, all of near pure gold are kept. High valued and gold-decorated dinnerware, golden utensils, high-grade brass and diamond studded artifacts are also kept in various boxes. Scrolls contained in golden tubes, where the history of Ancient Asian empires are written are also part of the inventory, several tin boxes were also listed containing gold bars of various sizes looted from Indian and Malaysian mining firms which at that time could easily fetch a value of a trillion US dollars. Indeed, the Empire of the Sun was able to hoard the treasures of Asia through the conquest of Yamashita, the Tiger of the Malayan Strait.

    Yamashita's escape plan was indeed about the successful arrival of the three trucks of treasures at the Japanese Imperial Palace. His intention is to use himself as a diversion so that the trucks of treasures will not be recovered by the Americans. He will then

Paul Roderick. A. Ysmael

make his main divisions visible and try to delay the advancing forces as much as possible. He shall then take the major roads so that his forces will be visible and the whole guerilla and American forces will concentrate on him. The mountainous terrain of the Cordilleras will be ideal for the protracted battle plan for the treasures' escape towards Japan. He thought that if the guerillas were able to use the mountains and its woods for their protracted revolution, his Japanese Imperial Army will also use the protracted strategy to effectively transport the treasure to Japan. The latest word from the Central Japanese Command in Tokyo was that the submarines which will fetch the trucks can only arrive in the Philippine northeastern coast by the last week of June at the earliest or first week of July at the latest. As the allied forces controlled the West Philippine Sea up to the Formosa Strait, the Japanese submarines were forced to use the Pacific Ocean sea lanes to reach the Philippines. Hence, the need to delay the advance of the USAFIP-NL forces until the submarines will be able to dock anywhere in northeastern Philippines. This explains the concentration of most Imperial commands in the Cordillera Region at the end of World War II.

Moha, and the other commanders were overwhelmed with awe and a sense of pride for having been selected to guard a treasure of such proportion. They were overjoyed by the trust of their Emperor. This feeling is typical of real Japanese warriors whose loyalty to their masters directly proportions to the trust given to them. The higher the level of confidence, the stronger their loyal ties to their masters. Moha even forgot the fact that he failed to report the loss of

Paul Roderick. A. Ysmael

the maps, copy of the treasure's inventory and other instructions to the guerillas. He listened intently to Yamashita's orders and instructions. Only ethnic Japanese soldiers will be allowed to guard the immediate perimeter of the trucks. They shall be sworn to defend then said trucks with their lives. The advance platoon will be the Korean conscripts and the Makapilis will be left to guard the town and the rear portion of the convoy. Moha is also instructed to as mush as possible move with speed and evade any detection or ambush. He should now vacate the garrison and let the Makapili occupy it as an interrogation area for suspected guerilla and sympathizers. Anyway, the guerilla forces may overwhelm the garrison with the decrease of his men as he had to heavily fortify the security of the trucks as they travel. He appointed Lt. Yamaha to initially command the security force immediately surrounding the trucks. Toki and Tomo each lead the platoons that will stay inside the said trucks.

By the first day of June 1945, Moha and his men officially became the guardian of the Emperor's Treasures. Moha was given a star for this mission, he became Brig. Gen. Moha. He commanded a phalanx of motorcycle mounted patrol that will guard the rear of his convoy, machine-gun mounted vehicles, five auxiliary personnel carrier, four patrol jeeps, weapons carrier, three light armor tanks, mortars, a light artillery and the armored personnel carrier that carried Moha and his immediate officers. To reduce

Paul Roderick. A. Ysmael

their load they left some boxes of treasures bars in the Yamashita cave.[2]

As the sun peeped beneath the towering Mount Namandiraan, the guardians of the hoarded treasure, set their journey to bring the trucks of treasures to Japan amidst the raging war at the bosom of the Cordilleras.

---

[2] Sometime in June 1977, a group of Japanese "tourists" riding in two buses with guides wearing IDs issued by Malacanang Palace, and guarded by a military truck with only seven soldiers went to visit the Yamashita cave, it was rumored that while the Japanese tourists were distributing Japanese, candies, noodles, ball pens and "friendship t-shirts" about twenty men were digging several boxes inside the Yamashita cave. They loaded the boxes in the military truck and when all their packages are ready, the buses sped off. Locals who went to the cave the following day were able to find old silver coins, around five small tin boxes which were already dilapidated by rust, Japanese Samurai (still displayed inside the cave) and other war artifacts that appeared to have been dug out.

Paul Roderick. A. Ysmael

Chapter Nine: The First Pursuit

Maj. Marcial Esguerra has always believed that the reason for the Japanese to concentrate their forces in the Cordilleras is due to the presence of the fabled Asian treasures in the area. They were not simply guarding the escape route of Yamashita. They were waiting for instructions as to how they will bring the treasures to Japan. He believed that if Yamashita really wanted to escape he could have just passed through Bessang Pass, went straight to the Pacific coast and directly sailed towards Japan. Esguerra's mind was so sharp to analyze the actions of his enemy. The terrain of the Cordilleras would have been enough to delay any pursuit against Yamashita. The Japanese general did not need to fortify Bessang Pass, unless there is a reason to really meet and engage his pursuers. Volkmann never believed Esguerra , which worked either as an advantage or disadvantage to Esguerra's plan to recover the treasures. Because of Volkmann's disbelief, Esguerra had the comfort to plan and recover the treasures in his own way. If he succeeds, he can deliver the treasures to the Philippine Government to be used in reconstructing the Philippine economy which is now devastated literally to the ashes by the ongoing war. His youthful idealism overcame his personal intentions. With the legendary value of the treasures that may reach to a trillion US dollars, the Philippines will immediately become a major economic power after the war. A legacy that not even Churchill's victory against the Nazis can surpass. A legacy that destiny has given him

Paul Roderick. A. Ysmael

a chance to crack. On the downside, he knows he has limited firepower and men to overcome the security blanket placed by the Japanese. If indeed the treasure of that proportion is stored somewhere amidst the Hills of Bessang Natural Park, he needed more than a hundred men to recover the same. Esguerra however can utilize Volkmann's excitement in capturing Yamashita and the patriotic and nationalist sentiment of his men to compensate whatever he lacked in arms and men. Esguerra was determined to take the treasures at all costs for the sake of elevating the lives of his impoverished countrymen.

A month after the inferno raid against the Cervantes Garrison, Maj. Esguerra sent a team to scout and locate the Yamashita Headquarters in Bessang Pass. Fortunately, Cirilo Ysmael was already in the guerilla camp. Having hunted down the rare Cordillera deer and the mouse deer for the past 25 years in the Western Cordilleras, Cirilo volunteered to guide the scouting team in scouring the Bessang Pass area. He also volunteered information on the cave-like formation about three kilometers southeast of the pass which maybe an ideal military camp due to its strategic location and presence of abundant water supply from the Bessang Pass watershed. After five days in the woods of Bessang Pass the scouts returned to confirm that indeed the main command of the Japanese forces is located at the said cave formations and which is now called the Yamashita Cave. The scouts reported that the cave network is composed of about five cave-like formations three of them are interconnected by natural tunnels. Around the caves are several foxholes where machine gun on tripods, mortar and light artillery are located. The foxholes are covered with camouflage trenches and military tents. The scouts estimated that around five hundred soldiers guard the cave complex. They also reported that three huge trucks covered with various kinds of camouflage are parked just outside the main cave. The said trucks are being guarded twenty four hours by several military police.

Maj. Marcial Esguerra immediately assembled his men. Their plan is not to overrun the camp as it is really impossible. It is to penetrate it, get some treasures to prove their existence, retreat immediately and then convince Volkmann to help him recover them. He decided to use only a hundred men for the mission. In the morning of May 28, 1945, they left the guerilla camp and travelled for three days to reach the Yamashita cave complex. Seven scouts led the pack, he stayed at the middle of his main force and Carlitos Leiza guarded his rear. Travelling always inside the woods they were an invisible force, taking advantage of the night where they are most effective. They ate only pre-cooked rations and moved in silence disturbing only the air as they passed, preserving the formation of the grass and twigs as if no one passed but their spirits.

Around noon of June 01, 1945, Esguerra's men reached the Yamashita Cave Complex undetected, they visually scoured the area and found that the forces had increased. From the reported five hundred men, it appears that the main guard of Yamashita of about a thousand are now concentrated in the area. The set their binoculars at the main cave's entrance and were

Paul Roderick. A. Ysmael

surprised to see that the three huge trucks were already gone from the place where they used to park. Esguerra was quick to realize that the trucks are either hidden or are already sent away as indicated in its escaper route. He immediately dispatched Carlitos Leiza's platoon to pursue the trucks in accordance with the direction of the treasure's map in case they already left. Carlitos' men were the logical choice because they are the rear and therefore can maneuver immediately. He then instructed the remaining men to wait for the night beneath the woods in order to enter the premises of the camp and search for the trucks under the cover of darkness. They maintained their silence and invisibility as they patiently waited for the proper time.

Quick and invisible, Carlitos reached the Maggoon viewpoint in a matter of an hour. The Viewpoint gives a panoramic and unobstructed view of the winding trail from Bessang Pass to the town of Cervantes. He however failed to see the convoy of trucks which by that time were resting near the Tamaang Creek covered by the lush vegetation of acacia trees and maguey shrubs. The pursuing platoon only saw an empty winding road with some Japanese soldiers patrolling with their military jeeps. Carlito's sent one of his men to report to Marcial Esguerra that nothing is significantly unusual in the highway trail. Esguerra, however, instructed them to continue their pursuit and follow the direction of the map. They can either stage an ambush in case the trucks will be dispatched or they can be a pursuing contingent if the trucks are already on the road towards the Mountain Province.

Paul Roderick. A. Ysmael

Carlitos Leiza asked permission to be allowed to employ all tactics in his pursuit which Esguerra granted. Realizing that the trucks may have been dispatched earlier than their arrival, he planned to commander a vehicle in order to improve their speed. He took with him seven of his men and went near the road to set up a roadblock near the Malaya Curve, around 15 kilometers away from Bessang Pass and 12 kilometers away from the Yamashita cave.

Around 1300HRS of the same day, a cruising Japanese patrol jeep stopped at a distance of around ten meters from the roadblock. Only three soldiers including the driver were on board. As the driver attempted a U-turn, Leiza and tree of his men, who were on a tall pine tree, jumped inside the jeep, cutting the throats of all the passengers and took control of the vehicle. They wore the uniform of the Japanese soldiers, disguised their men as Makapilis and set to pursue the trail of treasures in their own way.

Ten minutes later, they accidentally caught up with the tail of Moha's convoy which just finished eating their lunch near the Tamaang Creek. Recognizing that it is a Japanese military jeep, two patrol motorcycles approached Leiza's jeep. They shouted Japanese passwords which the guerillas did not understand. Still, the motorcycle patrols approached them. Leiza quickly ordered the driver to reverse and go back as the motorcycles have light machinegun mounts on their side cars. The motorcycle gunner fired warning shots, Leiza fired back as they retreated towards a trail at the right side of the highway. He was fortunate to hit the gunner's arm.

Paul Roderick. A. Ysmael

The other motorcycle started firing directly at them as they sped of inside a sugarcane plantation. They hid inside the plantation and prepared to ambush the pursuing rear patrol.

Moha, the commander of the convoy, was alarmed by the exchanges of sporadic gunfire at the rear portion of his convoy. He ordered his men to speed up. The third truck has been overloaded and cannot pace with the other two. In accordance with the instructions of Yamashita, Moha instructed Tomo to reduce the truck's load by unloading some of the boxes. Whatever will be left will be recovered by their forces and they will sell it to buy some supplies. Tomo and four other soldiers threw two small boxes of gold bars in a shallow ravine. Another soldier threw a grenade in order to let the ravine cave-in to cover the gold bars with soil and rocks.[3] They then sped off to catch up the other two trucks. This was how the boxes of Japanese gold bars were hidden in the Cordilleras, this explains why all known discoveries of gold bars were made near the main road from Bessang Pass to Mankayan, Benguet and in several parts of Halsema Highway.

Meanwhile, Leiza and his men were still in an ambush position three hours after the short gun-battle with the motorcycle patrol. They also took that time to rest for a while as they have been walking in the woods non-stop for two days and a half. When they no longer heard the humming of the motorcycle engines, they

---

[3] These boxes were discovered early 1984, when a group of men, Japanese and Filipinos, using a vehicle with markings of the "Ministry of Agriculture" dug it up, pretending to conduct soil analysis of the , Tamaang Valley Rice lands.

Paul Roderick. A. Ysmael

decided to move back into the main road, trying to follow the trucks of treasures.

Hours later, the Yamashita cave was already covered with fog, at nearly dusk, the place darkened as the sun finally hid behind the large cumulus clouds that rose from the Western seas. The lighting only came from bamboo torches and small battery powered bulbs that left much of the cave's outside and inside premises as dark as the forest night. The guerillas began moving slowly in order to search the place amidst the tired and weary Japanese force scattered around. Esguerra ordered Fungway and Anacleto to try squeezing themselves into the main cave to look at the commander's chamber while he got three other bolomen to search the other parts of the cave. He also formed an extraction force in case he and the others are trapped inside the cave. Their mission is not to hurt anyone, just to know where the trucks of the hoarded treasures are. Fungway and Anacleto used every box, curled rope, gasoline drums and other scattered materials as camouflage. The two literally crawled like snakes until they reach the main chamber of the Yamashita cave. Without any sound, defeating the silence of moving feline, they used their senses of touch and hearing rather than their eyes in roaming around the place. After fifteen minutes of fast and precise crawling from their initial positions, they were able to enter the commander's main chamber. Spartan and crude in all its aspects, the commander's chamber is poorly lit by a single bulb, the furnishings are composed of a military cot bed, several folding chairs, a makeshift table, a plywood where several Manila papers are being used for writing several notes mostly

Paul Roderick. A. Ysmael

in Japanese characters and numerical numbers. Then they saw a tin box covered with military uniforms and green textile. There were also rolled tents, sleeping bags, military sword and a pistol hanging around. The commander was nowhere in the chamber but two drowsing sentries are guarding his bed. In fact, the sentries looked bored, sleepy and tired that their alertness is suspect. Although, the crawling figures are really invisible from an untrained eye, their physical condition contributed to their failure to secure the place from the intruders. Adjacent to the chamber is a low but long table with two low makeshift benches made out of cut pine trees. The crudely made table appeared to be like a war table as several papers and pens are scattered. There were also rifles lined up at the walls of the cave but the intruders cannot see them as they are forced to be in a lying position. Anacleto was able to crawl beside a tin box, about five inches tall, two feet long and a foot wide. Without looking inside, he dipped his hands, and he felt several small but heavy bricks. Immediately he took a brick without looking and placed it in his pocket. He felt that the brick's weight dragged his trousers. He estimated that the brick weighed a kilo or less. He again dipped his other hand and took another brick, then crawled away from the box as Fungway watched his back. The two then retreated towards their position in the woods but kept themselves low as possible until they reached their point of rendezvous, occasionally crawling and covered by the relative darkness.

While Fungway and Anacleto were busy. Esguerra and his two companions searched the other parts of the cave, silently crawling like serpents. They

Paul Roderick. A. Ysmael

crawled into one of the cave's tunnels leading to what appeared to be a store room which is located beside the "war room." They estimated that the supplies can still feed more than a thousand soldiers in a week's time. Esguerra thought of burning the supply room but he was sure his whole force will be annihilated if the Japanese are roused from their sleep. So he just took the opportunity to spy on the logistical capacity of the enemy. He just took note of the ammo, food supplies and estimated forces in the camp. He then dispatched two bolomen to give his intelligence report to Col Volkmann. This information was vital in Volkmann's success in his last major attempt to conquer Bessang Pass.

Convinced that the trucks of their desire are already gone, Esguerra and his men retreated slowly while the enemy is resting. He then ordered his men to enjoy the remaining hours of the night to sleep. They will just regroup at the first light of dawn to plan their pursuit for the trucks of treasures. Esguerra was already contacting Carlitos about the report on the latter's reconnaissance operations. He planned to formulate an appropriate strategy from the said report.

As if on cue, Carlitos also paused for a while in his pursuit. He ordered their vehicle to stop at an abandoned hut near the Villanueva Ranch located south east of the town proper where they slept. The hut was built on an elevated slope, giving them a clear view of the sleeping town proper. Their location is already around three kilometers from the garrison enough for them to run away from enemy pursuit in case of adverse detection. At his strategic point he can

Paul Roderick. A. Ysmael

also view the Comillas North plains and also the Amburayan trail or the Bontoc-Cervantes Road. His vantage point would soon become a disadvantage as the confidence built by his post will be the sole reason for a successful deception from a cunning enemy.

Paul Roderick. A. Ysmael

Chapter Ten: Blazing the Golden Trail

Moha temporarily set camp in a foothill at the mouth of the Hacienda Moreno in Comillas North, heading towards the Ilocos-Benguet border. The hacienda at that time was deserted by its Spanish owners because the Japanese and the Makapilis considered them as guerilla supporters. We should not forget that one of the owner's sons, Angel Moreno is a guerilla leader and regular officer who commanded the Cervantes guerilla contingent. The hacienda temporarily became an agricultural plantation manned by Japanese and Makapilis. Its products were used to supply the needs of the Japanese forces operating in Bessang Pass and to those encamped at the Cervantes Garrison. In that location, Moha was about half an hour away from the pursuing team of Leiza. The place was ideal for encampment. The mouth of the hacienda is shrouded by acacia trees and tall sunflowers that abound the Benguet trail. Moha and his convoy were invisible from the vantage point of Leiza. Having been assigned in the area for the past three years, Moha has a dependable knowledge on the terrain. The Japanese soldiers likewise camouflaged themselves with wild vines and shrubs to enable them to have a short rest and evade detection. Its rear company set camp around two hundred meters away. They parked the trucks near Moha's armored personnel carrier for added security. As of now they are concerned with some bandits engaged in robbery in the mountain trail, but this is not a threat of whatever proportion. Moha's troop of five hundred armed men can easily

Paul Roderick. A. Ysmael

outgun and outnumber any bandit group of twenty to fifty. At the most, the bandits will only steal some food and ammunition from his perimeter guards. In fact, a few minutes into his sleep, Moha was awakened by three successive shots from a pistol. Indeed, a band of around ten men in g-strings attempted to steal some rations from the sleeping perimeter guards. One bandit was killed instantly and received all the three rounds from a young lieutenant's Luger .45. The nine others escaped unharmed taking only a box of canned goods with them. While dismissing it as a mere disturbance, Moha realized their vulnerability in the dark. He ordered additional night patrols, scattered more men to expand the perimeter defense and instructed the treasure guard to have a 24/7 alertness.

This is the second day of their journey, he had to maintain his pace as instructed. If they arrive early in the eastern coast, they will be an easy prey of the Hukbalahaps operating in the Sierra Madre region. If they are late and they will force their submarines to wait for a long period, they maybe detected by the American mine sweepers and warships operating in the Pacific. Precision is the key to their operation. So far, he just lost two men from the shootout the day before. He then summoned Lt. Yamaha and the other commanders for a briefing on their next days ahead.

He told them to keep the three trucks together for easier security. Tomo informed him that the load of each truck is too heavy for their engines and it is causing unnecessary fuel consumption. If they continue with that load, their gasoline may not be enough for their entire trip until Palanan, Isabela. In

Paul Roderick. A. Ysmael

fact, Tomo said that they are being forced to give some fuel to the three dummy trucks that will be going to the Kayan-Cervantes Road, in order to divert the pursuing guerilla forces that they encountered the day before. The said trucks will be filled with rocks and stones to simulate the weight of the real trucks of treasures. To further increase their semblance with the real ones, they will be transferring some boxes that are similar to the tin boxes. They will also be heavily guarded to instill the impression that they are the real ones. It will also divide the pursuing forces and it would be easier to neutralize them if necessary. To lessen their load, they took out several boxes of gold bars, scattered them in at least four places along their way to Buguias, Benguet.[4]

By that time, Moha is fully aware that a group inside the Philippine guerilla front has knowledge of the existence of the trucks of treasures. This is proven by the attack on the Cervantes Garrison which real objective is to steal the escape map of the trucks of treasures and the inventory records of the treasure. He formed a reconnaissance team to verify his suspicions. He sent the young Lt. Yamaha to the Makapili headquarters and with the assistance of the said Makapilis, they were able to verify that a guerilla force of about three hundred men composed of regular guerillas and bolomen are hell-bent on looking for the trucks of treasures. Indeed, the February 15, 1945

---

[4] Treasure hunters were able to locate only one of these four sites. They found four gold bars and several pieces of golden coins with Arabic inscriptions contained in a short circular drum near the Abatan, Buguias-Mankayan boundary, in Benguet province in 1979. These means that three locations are still being hunted until today.

Paul Roderick. A. Ysmael

raid is intended to steal the documents about the treasures in order for the guerilla officers to verify their existence at the hands of the Japanese Imperial Army in the Philippines. In fact, Moha also got a Makapili asset who convinced him that his friend Fungway is a long-time intelligence officer and that Benita is Fungway's assistant. Feeling betrayed, Moha gave instructions to Yamaha to punish everyone who transgressed Imperial Japan and decided to maintain a command in Cervantes for that purpose.

After learning this information about Fungway and Benita, Yamaha on his own and with five of his Korean conscripts went to the house of Benita Lang-ay about a hundred meters north of the Church of Cervantes. Fortunately, Benita is no longer around as she is already in the guerilla camp. However, they arrested her foster parents, tortured his foster father, Roberto Namita and the Koreans took turns in raping her foster mother Nenita, forcing them to tell her whereabouts. Eventually the two middle-aged couple succumbed to water torture inside the Cervantes Garrison. They joined the thousands of civilians who perished and were sacrificed in order for us to gain freedom from the wicked Japanese aggression and abominable cruelty that they committed in this part of the world. Yamaha then issued a manhunt order against Fungway, Benita, Cirilo Ysmael an all their supporters and sympathizers. He appointed himself the new commander of the Cervantes Garrison as Moha was busy running away with the trucks of treasures and the "dummy" convoy was being chased at the Cervantes-Bontoc Road.

Paul Roderick. A. Ysmael

Inflamed by their impending defeat at Bessang Pass, Yamaha instigated interrogations of suspected guerilla sympathizers. Men, young and old, mothers, virgins and children were being hauled into the garrison dungeon. Most never found alive, a few were rescued after the fall of Bessang Pass. But the carnage went on for nearly a month. Those who perished may have been luckier than those who survived the torture and rape and lived with them in turmoil, trauma and shock. The trauma was so revealing that they cannot even recall those memories. Their sad tales were only repeated with some degree of understatement by those who witnessed but lucky to have not suffered their ordeals. Then when Carlitos Leiza managed to ambush his convoy near the garrison, Yamaha began interrogating even the Makapilis and their families whom he suspected to be traitors. When Yamaha raped a young daughter of a Makapili, the Makapili father went berserk, he entered the garrison firing at everybody and managed tom wound Yamaha's ear, however, before he fired his fatal shot, he was cut into pieces by machinegun fire and as his last suffering, five bullets from Yamaha's pistol all at his forehead.

Meanwhile at the guerilla front, Marcial Esguerra received a report from Carlitos that the trucks of treasures have changed course. From their original route using the Mankayan trail, they turned left and used the Bontoc-Road. Because of the exact and vivid descriptions of the trucks, Esguerra relied heavily on the scouting report. He got all his available ammo, mines and explosives and commanded his men to cut and ambush the convoy using the north plank by rushing through the Quirino-Bontoc

Paul Roderick. A. Ysmael

Boundary north of the road and meet the convoy at Kayan, Mountain Province, the first town and town before Bontoc. To do that, they should not stop walking for three consecutive days, sleep for a few hours then instigate an ambush. And so, for three days and four nights, Esguerra and his men were literally running after the three dummy trucks. Moha's deception worked. He was able to confuse his pursuers.

Paul Roderick. A. Ysmael

Chapter Eleven: Empty Trucks of Treasures

After walking and running for three days and four nights on the rugged mountain ridges from Cervantes to Bontoc in the northwestern Cordilleras, Esguerra and around 250 of his men reached the Bontoc-Kayan border. They are now five kilometers ahead of the convoy. To reach that place, they ate their food while running and drunk water while walking. They seldom talked to preserve their strength for walking and not waste it by laughing or shouting. They were as silent as the civet that are endemic in the area. The eagle owl watched them as they passed by. There travel was so fast but very silent that they did wake up the hanging giant fruit-bats that are enjoying the warmth of the day while hanging atop the short macopa fruit trees that abound in the area. They are so focused that they did not mind being cut by the sharp thorns of wild cherries and bamboo along the way. Even the presence of vipers and attacking wild boars were ignored. They just killed a couple of boars for them to eat before their planned attack.

Esguerra sent Anacleto and another boloman to scout the convoy while he instructed his men to move farther ahead so that they can have time to rest before the attack. They were expecting the Japanese convoy to sleep during the night, if so, they will also take a nap to regain some strength before attacking. It has been a non-stop travel by foot for three days. Esguerra knows that most of his men are consumed by fatigue and lack of sleep. An hour of

Paul Roderick. A. Ysmael

short nap will spell the difference of the impending battle. Before sleeping however, Esguerra made an inventory of his personnel and ammo. He got enough explosives to blow the roads but sparing the trucks, he got five .30 caliber mounted machineguns sufficient to withstand half-day of fighting, several mortars and two artillery support. Every squad has a Browning Automatic rifle that can match up enemy machine gun fire. They had hand grenades. He got around 200 fully armed men and around twenty ladies acting as auxiliary-medical force, including Benita, who has since joined the guerilla force just after their escape from Cervantes. Around a hundred bolomen armed with only with bolos and home-made pistols will act as their explosives and medic teams. He knew he can match the convoy one by one. He then called his platoon commanders and gave his order of battle. Then they retired to their short sleep.

Meanwhile the Japanese dummy convoy was comfortably resting around five kilometers away from the ambush force of Esguerra. Their commander gave instructions to have a rear blocking force several kilometers away from the main convoy in order to keep Carlitos and his band at bay. The commander thought of just finishing off the band but had second thoughts because it is really their purpose to be tailed and lure the main force to run after them. If they annihilate the band, then they will prematurely engage the main force of the guerillas and their diversion will be discovered early. It was their plan to maintain Carlitos' pursuit until sufficient time has elapse to allow Homa to reach Isabela or Ifugao. By that time, there will be no way that the guerilla force can catch up the trucks

Paul Roderick. A. Ysmael

of treasures. Hence, related to their escape plan, they were deliberately slow in moving so that in case the guerilla force will attack them their distance with the real trucks will be sufficient. So at that time, they decided to stay put and made temporary camp and stay at the place for around twelve hours. The Japanese forcibly got two cows from a local farm in Barrio Aluling, located near the Cervantes-Kayan border, roasted it and had a feast with some drinking of a local rice wine. Drunk and filled up, they decided to sleep for the whole night. This gave Esguerra's force additional time to rest and extended their wait. Meanwhile Homa was already near the Benguet-Mountain Province Boundary on the other side of the mountains and in a different road. If pursued by Esguerra, Homa's force is about two days ahead and moving.

That was already June 10, 1945, the tenth day of the pursuit for the trucks of treasures. At Bessang Pass at that time, the fiercest fighting was ongoing. Yamashita, in a bid to delay the advance of the main armed force of the USAFIP-NL employed all his remaining divisions despite the advances made by the allied force. That time the allied forces already captured the advance base of the Japanese in Hill 94, above Butac, Suyo, Ilocos Sur. The main allied force is already in Naiba, five kilometers below Bessang Pass but a small group of Filipino guerillas led by a veteran of the Bataan Death March, Quirico Anga-angan has already breached the enemy lines and were already in Bessang Pass. They were already scouting the enemy at a distance of around one kilometer only. In June 11 of the same year the bloodiest Battle of Kumyeng,

Paul Roderick. A. Ysmael

occurred. Kumyeng is a narrow pass carved out of a rock-mountain just below Bessang Pass. The mountain has no vegetation being a rock mountain and the carved road has the steepest and deepest ravine in the area. It is a bare trail wherein the battling forces can only engage each other either on a face to face or hand-to-hand combat otherwise one has to run away. On that day, after taking the advance post, Volkmann gained confidence that they can defeat the enemy by continuous and relentless pursuit so that they will have no chance to regroup, get ammo and rest. He feared that giving the Japanese forces a reprieve will just prolong the battle and will cost him more lives. So on June 11, 1945, the allied forces and guerillas forces their way through Kumyeng trail. They massed about five hundred men, braving mortar and machinegun fire. Their first advance caused them around fifty lives and a hundred wounded but these lives and wounds were necessary to get Bessang Pass. On the second day they are now in front of the Japanese foxholes, engaging the enemy face-to-face, displaying their knife fighting skills, and overwhelming the enemy post. The Battle of the Kumyeng Trail is the most violent and the site of fiercest hand to hand combat ever witnessed by both forces in World War II. After two days of battle, both sides lost around two hundred men mostly by stab wounds and strangulation. By June 13, 1945, the allied forces are now knocking at the gateway of Bessang Pass. The Bessang pass was recovered by the Allied Forces on June 15, 1945.

Well rested and recently fed, the Japanese diversionary convoy decided to advance further into the east as slow as possible in order to wait for the main force of the guerilla forces that were pursuing them. While they succeeded in deceiving their pursuers, they underestimated their speed. Hence, they are on a wait and ambush attitude with the intention of delaying their pursuers and eventually meeting their comrades in Ifugao on the way to Palanan, Isabela. Their intention is to stay within northern Mountain Province for the next ten days or until June 20, 1945 and then rush towards Ifugao upon information that Homa's main forces will now be there. It was the farthest in their minds to think that Esguerra's men are waiting for them around three to four kilometers ahead. This frame of mind gave them a relative laxity and questionable alertness.

Esguerra on the other hand positioned his men in a sharp and ascending curve around three kilometers away west of the Bontoc Town Center. He feared that there might be a small Japanese contingent in the town of Bontoc which might delay their purpose. After three hours of wait or around seven o'clock in the morning, they already saw the advance forces of the Japanese convoy. It composed of a light tank, around five motorcycles with side car, each with light machinegun. They readied their mines, gasoline barrels and machine guns. His orders were to fire and blast off the enemy upon seeing the three trucks of treasures.

Thirty minutes later, the three trucks of treasures followed by two light tanks were about to ascend at the sharp curve. By that time the advance force of the convoy was only around fifty meter away

Paul Roderick. A. Ysmael

from them. The area was a picture of nature's beauty as the initial rays of sunshine were touching the moist grass of the wide Bontoc Valley. Only occasional crowing of cocks are joining the humming of the engines of the various military vehicles of the convoy. The parading military hardware and uniformed soldiers had an ironic backdrop of a peaceful valley with clear blue sky and lush greenery. There was an unusual silence and an eerie calmness engulfed the air. The Japanese commander marveled at the scenic bamboo clusters and thick vegetation of madre cacao shrubs surrounded by blooming sunflowers that characterized the vibrant Cordillera landscape. He was about to share his awe to his deputy, but before he can move his lips, he heard a loud bang! He felt something pierced his throat, fell down and forced himself to raise his head for the last time. The commander smiled as he looked at the rising sun which ironically faded like a sunset. It was the longest one second in his life. The mine instantly killed him.

    Esguerra saw how the armored personnel carrier carrying the Japanese commander was blasted to pieces. He just firmly held his Thompson and aimed at the advancing forces, some of them are now few meters from his position. The firing from each side was incessant. Five more blasts followed the initial mines. Ten barrels of gasoline were rolled to meet the roaring tanks. Their rear which housed their ammo boxes turned into time bombs exploding into the air, lifting the armored vehicle to a height of more than twenty feet. The Battle of Bontoc disturbed the peace of the vibrant valley. The incessant volleys of fire resulted to the atrocious smell of burning blood and skin. The

Paul Roderick. A. Ysmael

cocks stopped crowing, the birds went into wild indiscriminate flight to avoid being caught into the cross-fire. One by one the parading Japanese and Koreans, without a commander to guide them and with nowhere to hide, either fell or ran away. Hiding behind the hunky acacia trees, a handful of villagers silently watched with fear. These villagers will soon be the mouthpiece of this historical occurrence in this side of the Cordillera, in the years that will come. Thirty minutes later, the bolomen already climbed the burning trucks of treasures. Two hundred Japanese and Koreans lay dead as the Makapilis scampered to safety, some surrendering to the guerilla forces. Esguerra's forces suffered ten wounded, no casualty. Precision and flawless execution has always been the trademark of every ambush that was conducted by Esguerra's men. His explosives unit is led by the finest in the whole allied forces in the Philippines being graduates of the UP College of Engineering. His riflemen are alumni of the UP Rifle and Pistol Team, the most admired marksmanship club outside the Philippine Special Forces until today. It was therefore unusual for the Battle of Bontoc to be the most victorious and precisely executed ambush in the whole of World War II.

Esguerra led the opening of the trucks rear loads. His victorious laughs turned into immediate frustration as he saw steel pipes, used ammo shells, stones and empty treasure boxes inside each truck. He was not even happy to the report that they recovered around ten treasures bars inside one of the tin treasure boxes. Not losing his temper despite his manifest frustration, Esguerra lined up all those who

Paul Roderick. A. Ysmael

surrendered and instructed his deputy, Fabian Ver to interrogate them. He then asked the help of the tribal leaders to bury the dead with specific instructions not to desecrate their remains. He summoned a Belgian Catholic missionary priest who was stationed in Bontoc at that time to give the dead their final sacrament whether they are Catholics or Buddhists as long as they receive their final blessings. He also asked his security platoon to give military honors. After the burial of the enlisted men, Esguerra led the full military and heroes' burial to the officers whom he identified through their insignias. He singled out the Japanese commander and gave him a posthumous commendation which by this time still engraved on the commander's tombstone: "A rare jewel of the Japanese Imperial Army, whose only fault is his obedience to his superiors' orders and who has fought gallantry with honor and bravery." He was Lt. Colonel Alfonso Masaki Mamoto. Born in California to a diplomat and a housewife, and was repatriated to Japan during the outbreak of the war to join the Imperial Army. He was a veteran in the conquest of Malaysia and the Strait of Singapore where he got his promotion as major. He also joined in the campaign to drive away the Americans in Corregidor commanding an artillery batter until he was transferred to Northern Luzon to command a battalion guarding Bessang Pass until his final assignment as assistant to Col. Moha. He died admiring the rising sun, a fitting death to a real warrior who has excellently served the Empire of the Sun.

After the fitting ceremonies for his dead enemies, Esguerra sent a couple of men to meet Carlitos and

Paul Roderick. A. Ysmael

inform him to go back to the Halsema Highway. It was already ten o'clock and the gentle sun has already turned into a burning volley of fire, slowly warming the hot valley of Bontoc. He instructed Carlitos to scout for the real trucks of treasures. He then assembled his men, inspected the wounded and ordered them to rest for a day in Bontoc. His intelligence squad is interrogating those who surrendered. Cirilo Ysmael and his farm workers followed the guerilla forces in Bontoc and delivered rice and other food items including cigarettes, beer and canned goods which they got from the USAFIP-NL Headquarters in Suyo, Ilocos Sur which they transported via the Angaki-Abra- Bontoc Road. They had replenished the supplies to last for another month.

Fabian Ver, then a young fresh college graduate of the State University was Esguerra's main interrogator and intelligence officer. Stern-looking, mild mannered and soft-spoken, he was fit for his job. He was given a rank of Captain which he carried over from his ROTC rank. He was able to confirm Esguerra's suspicion that the trucks are somewhere in the Halsema Hi-way on the other side of the Mountain Province mountain range. They estimate it to be around three to four days away from them if they will follow through the highway on foot. They decided to start looking for the real trucks after taking their dinner that night. The Japanese maybe allowed to escape, but not with their trucks of treasures!

Paul Roderick. A. Ysmael

Chapter Twelve: The Final Pursuit

The Battle of Bontoc occurred just a day after the Battle of Kumyeng or on June 12, 1945. By that time, the allied forces have consolidated their hold in the Western and Northern Luzon. On June 14, 1945, the US Air Force already occupied Loakan Airport in Baguio City and the US Sixth Army re-occupied Camp John Hay. With the US Navy's Fleet stationed at nearby Poro Point in La Union, the Americans were able to consolidate a complete military force with air, sea and land component that no nation in Asia can match even years later. The American High Command set up a communications station inside Camp John Hay in order to ensure the coordination of their operations. The said communications station later became the broadcast station of the Voice of America. In other words, they made the camp their command headquarters for their Northern Luzon operations. After landing in Lingayen Gulf, General Douglas Mac Arthur went directly to Baguio City via Kennon Road. He held office inside Camp John Hay, which became his home until General Yamashita was captured. The command headquarters was receiving orders directly from the Pacific Command in Pearl Harbor. During that time, the American intelligence community were able to verify that indeed, General Yamashita was travelling with three trucks of treasures that he wanted to send to his Emperor in Japan. These treasures were the product of the Japanese campaign in India, Malaysia, and Thailand. Intelligence reports gathered from their operatives infiltrating the British

Paul Roderick. A. Ysmael

forces in China and India were able to trace the origins of the treasures and other precious artifacts. The Japanese hauled and hoarded them from various holy temples all over Asia. In fact, documented reports point Fort Santiago[5] in Manila as the storage of the treasures. This document is still in the archives of the US Central Intelligence Agency until the present day. Several treasure hunters have a copy of this report and this is the reason why foreign and local treasure hunters will be haunting Fort Santiago after the war. This intelligence information was sent via telegram to General Mac Arthur together with confidential orders as to how will the American forces will deal with the golden hoard. Years later, treasure hunters will claim that they have copies of this directive as they attest on the truth of the trucks of treasures.

Meanwhile, in Bessang Pass, General Yamashita already left his natural fortress and has already used the Bakun, Benguet trail to catch up with Col. Moha. His instruction was to inflict the most damage against the pursuing allied forces within their remaining capability in the night of June 14, 1945 . Yamashita ordered his men to use all their ammos, leaving only what they need to escape and use the darkness of the night as cover for the retreat of all forces. So in the evening of that day artillery propelled shells relentlessly rained on the advancing forces.

---

[5] An American treasure hunter dug inside the historic Fort Santiago in Manila sometime in the year 2001 but he only found empty containers which may have housed gold bars and ancient jewelry. Media reports forced him to abandon his months of digging and there was no report of any successful hunt. This proves that the gold and treasures were transported out of Fort Santiago to a place somewhere outside the Metro Manila area.

Paul Roderick. A. Ysmael

Machineguns incessantly fired at all directions where the guerillas were advancing. The firing was so intense that even a short period of three seconds of hearing it will make you deaf. The casualty on the part of the advancing forces ran into hundreds. Every step of the advancing forces was met by mined trenches, barbed wires, hand thrown and ground grenades, machinegun fire and rockets. Many limbs and feet were blasted by cannons and mortars. Many bodies were halved by relentless rifle fire. The allied forces however were determined to get the Pass. The deathly passion of their ascension towards Bessang Pass was symbolic of the hardship and sacrifices that the nation suffered in order to regain freedom from Japanese domination (only to be put into waste by the corruption of Filipino political leaders' later on).

The hundreds of lives lost in just one evening represented the value of liberty and the cost of loving a country, whatever its future will be. For the bolomen who perished, they knew that their lives were their only valuables that they can contribute in rebuilding this Nation. To the regular soldiers, their gallantry and fearless assault were all the proof that they were gave to their country to prove that they are its true soldiers for its freedom and liberty. For the Americans, it is a vindication of their humiliating defeat in Corregidor and Bataan. The Battle of Bessang Pass was the only battle where they did not use their superior air power and naval assets. It was really a battle fought by men and not by metals. Enemies were not killed by flying bombers and blazing warships, a thousand feet above nor miles away from the sea. It was a battle where one literally faces his enemy.

Paul Roderick. A. Ysmael

It was a measure of who is the more superior among warring soldiers. Eye to eye, arms to arms. It was a test of bravery, toughness and fighting skills. It gave all the fighters the chance to face death and survive it, if you are the better person. The quest for ultimate manhood and masculinity was offered by the raging battle. For each of those men, the survivors and to those who perished, it was their longest minute, longest hours, and their longest three days. It was a battle that each participant can always call his ultimate fighting experience.

As instructed, the Japanese forces emptied their artillery batteries with incessant firing, when all the shells were spent, the remaining infantry left silently and quickly to catch up with the main force commanded by Yamashita. They emptied their machinegun ammo box and left.

So for three long hours, from five in the afternoon until eight in the evening, the twin peaks of Bessang Pass resembled a fuming volcano. It lit the whole of Western Cordillera with a brightness that was seen as far as Poro Point. La Union in the southwest and Candon City in the northwest. The US Navy's coastal patrol along the scenic Ilocos Coast saw the shining light on top of the Bessang Pass like a continuous volcanic eruption. The allied forces were forced to halt their advance due to the volume of fire and unexpected casualty for the said three hours. Unknown to them, the Japanese were firing their last cannon shells and final bullets. The Land of the Rising Sun was spewing its last imperial venom in Philippine soil.

Paul Roderick. A. Ysmael

When the clock struck eight in that evening, silence and darkness engulfed the mountain top. The allied forces considered the cessation of fire as a Trojan trap so they decided to wait for several hours. Fearing for mines, they decided to stay in their position and wait for the morning light. The rest of the night was only disturbed by intermittent sniper fire from both sides. The firing of rifles was more of announcing one's presence than intending to harm. The exchange of harmless shooting lasted until dawn. After the remaining Japanese soldiers spent all their magazines, they threw away their rifles and started the life of stragglers. Decades later, tens of Japanese will still be found wandering inside the forests of Bessang Pass Park.

Early in the morning, Volkmann sent his First Cavalry Company to climb into the Pass. It was led by a young red neck from Memphis, Tennessee named Capt. Michael Saulsberry. Composed of young and fearless men barely in their twenties, the company reached the pass with relative ease amidst a deafening silence. As they draw nearer to the of the five Japanese artillery batteries that guarded the pass until last night, they saw Japanese soldiers who were silently praying facing the rising sun. The Japanese were unmindful that their backs were against their advancing enemies. They were in full "dress grey" ceremonial uniforms each with a small flag of the rising sun neatly wrapped over their right arms. Saulsberry, whose men were already in firing position signaled a halt. He raised a "desist-firing" hand command. He waived his hands to calm his over-eager men and silently ordered them to just watch. As the

Paul Roderick. A. Ysmael

Japanese artillery men finished their prayer and still facing the sun, they simultaneously pulled their military swords upwards, with the pointed tips aimed towards their mid-sections. On cue, they shouted: "BANZAI NIPPON" all together, and on an abrupt but synchronized fashion, stabbed themselves until their swords pierced their bodies. Slowly they fell one by one, until their faces evaded the sun and their lifeless torsos hit the ground. In the tradition of Japanese samurai warriors they chose to die by their own sword rather than by their enemy's blade. This is one of the illustrations of the legendary Japanese "samurai" gallantry and patriotism during World War II. This is not different from Tora-tora pilots, dying with their planes, Japanese captains drowning with their submarines. Japanese artillery men died with the last cannon ball of their batteries.

That was the final and untold part of the Battle of Bessang Pass. Stunned and shocked, Saulsberry and his men froze for more than five minutes and then their eyes voluntarily shed their first tears of sorrow in their young lives.

Saulsberry then ordered Quirico Anga-angan's bolomen to prepare the burial for the Japanese artillery crew. He then rendered the Japanese full military honors for their heroic departure. During the years that will follow, hunters and night travelers will be talking about seeing the ghosts of these Japanese artillery men, who are dressed in light grey and standing while facing east, as they pass by that area at dawn, every 15th day of the month June.

Paul Roderick. A. Ysmael

Waiting for further orders, Sauslberry and his men set camp at Maggoon Hill, three kilometers away from Bessang Pass. The hill is strategically located as it provides an unobstructed view of the Cervantes Town Proper, especially on the Garrison. With powerful binoculars, they can observe the town which is about 20 kilometers away.

By that time, half of the remaining Japanese infantry men retreated towards the Cervantes Garrison. There they nursed the wounded and rested for a day. The other half continued on their journey towards the route of the trucks of treasures. Because of the casualties that his forces suffered, Volkmann decided to ask for aerial attack on the town center of Cervantes. This will spare the lives of his men and will expedite the war. He knew he had to continue his battle while still on a winning edge, but losing more than five hundred men in Bessang Pass was too much for him. He cannot risk fighting the enemy in the plaza without any aerial support. It will just prolong the battle and increase the cost on human lives, unnecessarily. So, on June 16, 2012, around a dozen B-54s, or what the Cervantes residents call "double-bodied airplanes" and several attack planes from the American carrier stationed in Poro Point, bombarded and strafed the town center of Cervantes, turning every building into dust. Immediately, the US Cavalry and aiding bolomen and guerilla forces surrounded the garrison. The Japanese and Makapilis surrendered without firing a shot. Saulsberry lined up the Japanese and the Makapilis in front of the garrison tied to each other. He then freed the remaining prisoners including one surviving American pastor

Paul Roderick. A. Ysmael

named Rev. Steven Foster who was then 75 years old. He turned over the prisoners to the local guerilla forces under the command of Angel Moreno and Quirico Anga-angan. The local leaders then conveyed to the guerilla forces their ordeals under the hands of the Japanese occupation commanded by Lt. Yumi Yamaha. With the crowed shouting about his atrocities, Lt. Yamaha was hanged. The crowd cheered in overwhelming approval. People will soon talk about seeing the hanged Japanese's ghost walking around the plaza with a rope tied around his neck and cursing pair of small eyes

Paul Roderick. A. Ysmael

Chapter Thirteen: Tracking the Trucks of Treasures

Fabian Ver's way of interrogation has always been long, circuitous and tedious. But he had the reputation to be an effective interviewer and an intelligence officer who always got his information. After lining up his prisoners composed of around ten Japanese, twenty Koreans and fifty Makapilis he led them into the parish house manned by the Belgian

Paul Roderick. A. Ysmael

Catholic Mission. He instructed the bolomen to prepare breakfast and invited his prisoners, to share the festive line of food composed of fried brown mountain rice, fried banana, boiled eggs, grilled sweet potato and dried cow's meat or the local "tapa." The bolomen managed to get a bottle of orange syrup from a church helper, mixed them with sugar and served it as orange juice. Ver jokingly said that no one among the prisoners can complain for maltreatment or any violation of the Articles of War or the International Humanitarian Law. "At least as of this time," he qualified, "you are being treated as humane as possible, as long as you please me." He then displayed a friendly grin and asked one young Makapili to say the Prayer before Meals. He started their breakfast by breaking a huge grilled sweet potato which he dipped in a molasses sauce. The captive followed suit and relieved their hunger with the steaming fried rice which was made aromatically tasteful by the spicy Ilocos garlic and a perfect match to the salty dried cow's meat. All the harshness of war were temporarily set aside by the warring men as they cherished the relief from days of hunger and thirst for water.

Midway in finishing his meal, Ver made an effort to place his prisoners to a certain level of comfort and acceptance. He relayed to them the latest update on the ongoing World War II. As he gnawed the hard dried meat, he showed them copies of the broadsheet Manila Bulletin, announcing the "Fall of Manila" with the headline "Manila Declared by America as Open City." To complement his story, he also narrated the latest news at Bessang Pass and apologizing for the lives of his captors' fallen comrades. He tried to show sincerity

Paul Roderick. A. Ysmael

and compassion to his captured enemies as possible as it can be. He said that everyone in the war is a victim. All are victims of their own principles and loyalties. He expressed understanding to the Japanese who were only doing their duty as subjects of their emperors, to the Koreans who were only forced via conscription to help their Japanese invaders, and to the Filipinos who betrayed their country because they believed that the hope of the Philippines lies in the hands of the Japanese.

"After the war, we do not know what becomes of each of us," he exclaimed, "we do not know if in the next war, the Japanese will already be the ally of the United States and the Filipinos are their enemies. The differences that our nations have are temporary. So, on a personal level, I hope, our differences will end today and let us start helping one another in rebuilding our country."

He said that in less than a year's time, the war will already be over and it would be best for them to start being friends. He urged his prisoners refrain from considering his questions as interrogation but rather a friendly exchange of information and ideas about the war and how to rebuild the Nation. He then asked one of the Makapilis about his plan after the war but the young man just gave him a stare. He then continued on his story as to how Japan has lost all its islands in the Pacific and of the bombing of the cities of Hiroshima and Nagasaki. Ver then waited for the comments of his prisoners.

The first prisoner to speak was the Japanese who spoke in fluent English. The Japanese apologized

Paul Roderick. A. Ysmael

for the war and for whatever Japan did against the Filipinos. However he said that the sufferings that the atomic bombs will inflict upon his people are undeserved. He said no human race whatever fault it may have committed deserves a punishment of nuclear proportion. Even Hitler's Germany was spared of an atomic annihilation. He said that he personally viewed the bombing of Hiroshima and Nagasaki as a racist act as the Americans spared the white Germans and elected to drop the dreaded bombs on an Asian soil. He said Japan's fault is its desire to build a state of cooperation among Asians but it may have gone to some extremes because of its alliance with the Nazis in Europe. Yet, with tears in his eyes, the Japanese reiterated : "No human being should experience the havoc and debilitating effects of an atomic bomb. In as much as we admit to have committed all our excesses in this war, from Manchuria to Malaysia to the extent of raping even homosexuals and fellow men in Manila, dropping a bomb that killed thousands of innocent civilians to end this war can never be justified."

He expressed concern more on the fate of the survivors who were infected by the radiation. No one knew at that time the effects of the bomb to the future generations of Hiroshima and Nagasaki. The conversation then dragged on as the prisoners began speaking and giving their opinions on the war in general, on the A-bomb and on their personal experiences. Ver patiently listened to each of them. He asked indirect questions whenever he had a chance to interrupt. While looking as if he was very concerned on the personal feelings of his captives, Ver was never distracted. He was determined to fish for the most

Paul Roderick. A. Ysmael

relevant information on the movement of their enemies and on the strength of their remaining forces. He wanted to fish in the most relaxing way. He knows that he is sailing above a sea of information but he opted for the peaceful manner rather than the violent way of "dynamite" fishing. Just like in real fishing expedition, the fish that you catch looks pleasant and complete if you catch it the peaceful way. If you use dynamite, you may catch the fish but it is either headless or blasted. Certainly if you use explosives, you will have a dead fish, while if you cast a net or use bait, you will get a live fish, complete and fully usable information. Of course, he knew his art of interrogation too well more than the art of actual fishing.

. Before they ate the last piece of their breakfast, Ver was able to get all the information that he wanted. Nearly each and every captive volunteered all information that they knew about the trucks of treasures. What is notable is Ver's ability to get all his information without resorting to torture or violence, a true mark of an intelligence officer.

As the Japanese officer narrated to Ver, the trucks of treasures are still on its route to Japan as stated in the original map. By that time, however, complications may have arisen as Yamashita's main force already abandoned Bessang Pass to catch up with the convoy of Col. Moha. This means a larger army now guards the periphery of the trucks of treasures. Their force of only around 250 healthy men may not be enough to repulse the convergence of Japanese forces. If they recruit other guerilla force and increase there numbers, they would be easily detected.

Paul Roderick. A. Ysmael

Besides of all the hundreds guerilla commanders, only Esguerra is convinced that there is such a thing like the trucks of treasures traversing the rugged roads of the Cordilleras. It is difficult to involve those who do not believe their cause. They may nave acceded Esguerra's invitation for the sake of friendship but the men may be half-hearted. Any additional force may only be a liability. In fact, they initially thought of recruiting their Filipino captives to join them but their long history of violence and revenge extending to personal level with the Makapilis is already a great reason to distrust them. Instead, they hauled their captives to the Bontoc Provincial Jail and cramped them in one detention building of one cell, designed only for twenty prisoners. They left a platoon of regular guerillas to guard them and a contingent of bolomen to augment their force. They designated Cirilo Ysmael as the temporary post commander of the Bontoc bolomen. He was instructed to feed the captives first before themselves and to ensure that they will be transported back to Manila or to the nearest American camp after the war. A day later, a contingent from the Cervantes guerilla camp of around ten men arrived to augment their armed force. They also transformed the provincial jail to be their temporary post while the Philippine-American Command has not yet organized a civilian government in the area. Cirilo then acted as a temporary civilian administrator of Bontoc for several months.

Meanwhile, Albert Fungway and Benita Langbay already reached the Barrio of Abatan 90 in the town of Buguias in the northeastern part of Benguet. Abatan 90 is designated as such because it is 90 kilometers

Paul Roderick. A. Ysmael

away from Burnham Park in Baguio. It is also called the "Abatan Junction" because it is where the junction for the roads leading to Mountain Province and Ilocos meet like a "Y-joint." They got a word that about three hundred soldiers with Japanese flags went towards Mountain Province and more have followed. They have trucks and tanks and some artillery pieces. According to their informant, there has been fighting also in the Benguet side as American forces from Baguio City encountered a Japanese advance contingent in Saddle Point, Sayangan, Atok, Benguet. The Americans are moving northward towards Buguias when they met the Japanese contingent from Bakun, Benguet. Bakun is the town adjacent to the Bessang Pass-La Union route which was being used by loggers and eventually, years later by alleged marijuana planters. It appears that the Japanese from Bakun served as blocking force of the main contingent of General Yamashita. Fungway wondered on the sudden interest of the Americans from Baguio City to move northwards considering that two days before, Bessang Pass has fallen into the hands of the allied forces and that Volkmann is now pursuing Yamashita in the mountains. He suspected that the Americans may also be in pursuit of the trucks of treasures! Immediately, he dispatched an asset to the location of Esguerra at the other side of the mountain. The asset, disguised as a coffee trader, used a reliable steed from Abra to traverse the rugged mountain trail.

The suspicion of Fungway is actually true. In fact, all the American ground forces, except the main force of Volkmann who was instructed to capture Yamashita, were in pursuit of the trucks of treasures.

Paul Roderick. A. Ysmael

After burying the Japanese artillery crew, Saulsberry's mounted cavalry received a direct order from their US Cavalry command post in Poro Point to proceed towards the Mountain Province area and leave Volkmann's forces. Their mission is to scout for three Japanese cargo trucks under the command of a certain Col. Moha and help the command to stop these Japanese forces from fulfilling their "special mission". According to their mission order, the force that they are looking is easy to identify as only Japanese soldiers were assigned to guard the trucks. Under strict orders, they were ordered not to engage the Japanese convoy, they will just inform the nearest command post as to the location of the convoy through their sophisticated radio equipment. That is the reason that they are only equipped with carbines and Thompson rifles, which were light to carry and made them very move fast. They will just act as a mobile reconnaissance force.

    The young Capt. Saulsberry took a native hog merchant from Barrio Malaya in Cervantes named Anastacio Gaburno and his son, "Ikoy," to serve as their guides in the wilderness of the Cordilleras. The Gaburnos knew the mountain provinces by heart as they are selling the rare black native pig with one white and three black paws which the Igorots used in their caniaw feasts. The Gaburnos also taught the Americans how to survive the wild, making fire and cooking rice using bamboo, eating the famous "mountain eel" or igat and dried horse meat. They acted both as human compass and a commissary for the American cavalry. Using the map issued by the US

Paul Roderick. A. Ysmael

Cavalry Command, Saulsberry proceeded towards Bontoc via the Halsema Highway.

Carlitos Leiza who by that time had set up camp in the boundary of Mankayan and Buguias, Benguet waiting further instructions from Esguerra was surprised when he saw Saulsberry's cavalry contingent. The cavalry was composed of around 120 men, all were Americans, around eighty of them, including all the platoon leaders were white. The remaining 40 are either are Afro-Americans or dark Mexican-looking soldiers. No Filipino guerilla was with them, indicating that the mission was also All-American in nature. He sent a word to Fungway who eventually informed Esguerra on the unexpected presence of the Americans in the area. Raw intelligence reports therefore have been confirmed. The Americans in the area are also in the hunt for the trucks of treasures. Esguerra then instructed his men to be more vigilant. Fungway was instructed to observe the Americans in the south who are going northwards, Carlitos was instructed to tailgate Saulsberry. Their main force which was still within the outskirts of Bontoc will try to intercept the main convoy of Moha along the Mountain Province-Nueva Vizcaya trail and expedite the recovery of the trucks. Everything was clearly understood by these men but in their heart they know how hard to accomplish their missions.

Meanwhile in Moha's convoy, they likewise received a word about the arrival of Yamashita in the Benguet area. They also heard about the fighting at Saddle Point. This caused them alarm and a reason to move faster than their usual pace. A day after, Moha

Paul Roderick. A. Ysmael

received instruction from General Yamashita to scatter the Golden Buddha and several boxes of gold bars in various parts of Benguet and Mountain Province. Moha was instructed to hide the said treasures in locations which are "near the road but with natural markers. The natural markets are identified as near century-old trees, major crossings and bridges. They have already hid some of these treasures in locations like these in Cervantes. Because of the annihilating effects of the bombing of Hiroshima, the plan of their Emperor changed. The Emperor wanted to surrender to the Americans, finish the war, accept whatever America mandates them to do in a peace treaty just like any loser in a war would, and get back the treasures latter. Moha was instructed to scatter the treasures as far as possible and try to bring to Tokyo only the Great Golden Komodo and those which the trucks can carry at ease. Moha was also instructed to make a map on the locations of the treasure, send an officer immediately to Tokyo with the Treasure Map who shall be fetched by a submarine first in the town of Baler at the Northern part of Tayabas. Complying with the directive, Moha ordered his men to make their trucks at least half-empty and dig shallow pits to hide the treasures near old trees, bridges, junctions, road and river crossings, old concrete buildings, large tombs and other easily identifiable locations. He left the Golden Buddha in Buguias, several boxes of gold bars in the Abatan Junction area and scattered them along the roads of Bauko Mountain Province. The Japanese commander even sent some treasures at the famous Sagada cave and placed the jewelry loot in earthen jar coffins and buried them at the deepest part of the cave. Today legend has it that these jewelry

Paul Roderick. A. Ysmael

pieces are located at the bottom of the lake inside the cave and guarded by the "Anitos." Moha then selected Toki as the officer who will bring the map to Tokyo. He was escorted by two veteran Japanese special forces sergeants and a Makapili guide. Toki broke into tears, he might survive the war but he had no chance to see his Benita before leaving. The love that he found amidst the flames of war will soon be burned into the ashes of lonely memories. He then left a note in a sari-sari store, a note more romantic and passionate than Mac Arthur's "I shall return." He did not give a promise to return to her, but he made a vow that Benita shall always be present in his heart, she is with him in this journey, he will always be in her dreams and he will never fall in love again. So Toki, with the treasure's location map left for Tokyo. No one knew at that time if he will ever make it.

Days later, all the armed groups inside the heart of the Cordilleras intensified their actions for the trucks of treasures. The pursuers both from the Filipino and American sides, doubled their efforts to locate the trucks, the Japanese on the other hand became invisible amidst the pristine pine forests, thick fog, late afternoon showers and the thick vegetation of wild sunflowers. They have intensified their efforts to transport and secure their treasures using the rugged terrain as their camouflage.

In July 02, 1945, Saulsberry's men caught up with a blocking force of Moha near the Bauko-Buguias boundary. Falling into a trap made by the Makapilis, Saulsberry with two of his men tailed a squad of Japanese soldiers. Unknown to them, the Americans'

Paul Roderick. A. Ysmael

presence were already reported to Moha by Makapili sympathizers in the area. Moha sent a squad to lure them into pursuit and then ambush or arrest them in order to gain information on the movements of the Americans. Tomo led around two platoons to "meet the Americans." They were able to spot the Americans resting in a roadhouse restaurant near the Abatan Junction enjoying the cold mountain breeze and hot local hamburgers. A second after establishing a vantage position, the whole Japanese platoon, in a swift military choreography fired at them and hurriedly retreated. They were able to wound a big black soldier standing around six feet and ten inches with a "body of an elephant." Young and relatively inexperienced, Sauslberry rode on his horse and led his troops in pursuit. All their carbines and Thompsons were blazing with silver bullets as their horses' hooves shook the ground. Tomo and his men ran as fast as they could to avoid being fired at by the raging Americans. They ran towards a deep descending curve towards Bauko town and just as they passed the blind curve, the Makapilis lifted a trapping rope that caught the left front leg of Saulsberry's black horse. The horse tumbled throwing Sauslberry about ten meters away and below the trail. The brown horse beside him suffered the same fate, the rider was also tossed down in a deep ravine. The rest of the Americans were able to stop and return back in order to avoid the Makapilis who were firing back at them. Saulsberry and an African-American trooper were caught captives by the Makapilis.

Observing atop a nearby hill, Leiza and his squad witnessed the skirmish and were surprised by

Paul Roderick. A. Ysmael

the limited battle skills of the American Cavalry. It was a short battle between wit and brute force. Wit includes the ability to control one's emotions. And the better brain had the edge. They contented themselves just learning from the short lesson of warfare. They cannot intervene nor participate as they were avoiding detection by both the Japanese and the Americans. They divided their squad into two and followed the captors of Saulsberry behind the bushes. The Makapilis tied their captives together. Over eager to "punish" a white man they occasionally boxed and kicked Saulsberry and hacked him with the butt of their rifles. He observed that the Makapilis were lenient on the black soldier. The said captives were led to the camp of the Japanese rear patrol pending instructions from Moha. Leiza was quick to realize that the Japanese will no longer intend to keep prisoners as they are in retreat. He pitied the young American who may have been in his first battle and too eager to fire his gun. This is the real risk among young officers who think that their West Point training and theoretical knowledge in warfare are enough to equip them in the battlefield. They forget that fifty percent of winning a battle is about knowing the terrain and the enemy. Fifty or sixty percent is luck! The young American officer may have refused to believe Sun Tzu's Art of War, perhaps he doubted its value because it is made in China.

Military training even in the best military schools does not contribute to the over-all chance of winning a battle. Once you are fired upon and start firing your gun, your chances entirely depend on your instincts and presence of mind. Leiza always

Paul Roderick. A. Ysmael

remembers what he read about the great Filipino Revolutionary General Antonio Luna, the best military tactician during the Filipino-Spanish War. Luna once told his men that in a battle, both sides knew how to employ military tactics and the men of both sides are also armed. Therefore, military training and even arms do not matter. Once the shooting starts, the better soldier is the one who can still think while the bullets are blazing an inch near your ear. If you can use your brain amidst the sounds of rifles, the tactics are simple. If you are lower, you try to go to a vantage point. If you transfer location, someone should cover you. Never fire your gun if the purpose is to expose your location. Fire if you have a chance of hitting. Once fear and nervousness engulf you, try pressing the trigger, once you fired the first shot, you will come to your senses again.

Leiza always shared this to their new recruits. In fact, he trains his men with live bullets to impress upon them that in a battle, fear to a rattling sound of a bullet is equivalent to death itself. It is every soldiers mission to avoid being hit unless necessary or unexpected.

Leiza realized that the young American may have graduated from the famous West Point. He knew how to ride his horse, he was excellent in handling his rifle, he was an officer and a gentleman in form, but forgot to manage his temper. Because of the age of the captured American officer, Leiza decided not to waste the life of this young man in these final days of the war. He signaled all his squad members to retreat into a nearby compound with an old acacia tree. They will

Paul Roderick. A. Ysmael

encamp there for the night. At that time, Saulsberry and his trooper were already tied in a wooden post. The Makapilis selected a post with an anthill made by the vicious red Cordillera ants whose eggs are sweet but their bites are the most painful in the whole ant-world. A thousand ants feasted on the legs, arms and faces of the captives. They were not offered anything, not a single drop of water or a grain of rice. They cannot even rest as they are tied on a tip-toe to ensure that they will be exhausted and weakened just by their condition. Occasionally, the Japanese sentries pass by them and give them either a kick or a slap, to ensure that they are still alive.

At a minute past midnight, the advance post was already asleep. Only a squad of sentries and the two captives were awake. It was dark and the only source of lighting are the ten makeshift torches made up of clothes soaked in kerosene and stuffed in beer bottles. This has been the light of the Cordillera town until the mid to late 1980s, when rural electrification stopped their 24-hour hour daily celebration of the Earth Hour. Such lighting is effective for an area of around ten square meters only. This is known by Leiza and his men who since birth were using such lighting. They already mastered how to be invisible in the darkness around such flames. They know how to synchronize their bodies with the flickering fire and appear like shadows of the light itself. So, like pythons, they crawled towards the American captives, within a distance to the light unseen by the sentries. Their phantom presence scared the ants which considered them as predators rather than prey. They were so effective that while they were untying the

Paul Roderick. A. Ysmael

hands and legs of the captives who were already asleep due to hunger and extreme exhaustion, three sentries were staring at their direction but they were invisible. As the tired eyes of the sentries moved to a different direction, they were already able to pull the captives away. In a wink of a sleepy eye, the rescuers and the captives are gone. In less than a minute, they are now outside the enemy camp. They did this with no sound so loud enough to be heard by the sentries, no movement that can be seen in the flickering light. It was so thrillingly precise. But most of all, they saved two lives without taking the life of anybody. They did not only give the prisoners their freedom, they gave them an extension of their young lives. The rescued Americans cannot say a word. They were awed by the skill of their rescuers that they cannot even utter any word to thank their rescuers. They just sighed as a sign of relief from the claws of certain death. It was already dawn when the Japanese discovered that their captives "escaped," wondering how and short of commending the Americans for such an excellent skill in escape and evasion. Years later, those who survived the war from the Japanese camp, will always be telling the tale of the two American officers. The two American captives, who suddenly became invisible before their eyes, and escaped under their watch.

In the morning following his rescue by "unknown" Filipino friends, Saulsberry was able to return to his men, badly beaten and hungry but free and happy. As an act of gratitude, he gave to Leiza his military saber which was awarded to him by the US West Point Military Academy for being best in his class. He also gave them ammo and some of their

Paul Roderick. A. Ysmael

reserved handguns, lighters and boxes of Lucky Strike. To avoid revealing their true mission, Leiza introduced himself to Saulsberry as among his captors who "decided to leave" the Japanese camp. They are some of the Filipino Makapilis who are returning to their lives as civilians for they knew the war is about to end. He then warned Saulsberry about the capability of the Japanese to set up traps and ambush attacks. He told them that the Japanese have obtained a mastery of the terrain in the area. There are mines and traps in the main roads to deter any pursuit. It would be best for them to just stay in a defensive position until they are ordered otherwise. Leiza and his men then left the Americans before daybreak. He however got the confirmation that Saulsberry was after the trucks of treasures. Indeed, truth comes from a heart beaming with gratitude! As he introduced himself as a defecting Makapili, Saulsberry asked him about the trucks of treasures. At first he feigned ignorance but the young American narrated to him, the legend of the trucks of treasures and his mission to locate, the said trucks of treasures. As Saulsberry confirmed, the American High Command and their Defense Department has confirmed that the treasures that the Japanese hoarded from Malaysia, Indonesia, India, and Thailand which are composed of golden artifacts, gold bars, old coins and precious stones were stored in Fort Santiago in Manila. When they liberated Manila, they searched all the tunnels, dungeons and all buildings located at Fort Santiago and in all buildings and churches that are inside the Walled City of Intramuros District but found no treasures unless you can consider the gold plated grail used by the Archbishop of Manila which they found inside the Manila Cathedral's sacristy area.

Paul Roderick. A. Ysmael

According to military intelligence, the treasures may not have been shipped out of the Philippines because all vessels were sunk by American bombardment. Civilian vessels that they thought of having just left the Port of Manila and nearby ports were all boarded and searched by the US Naval assets all over the West Philippine Sea. The Americans were also confident on the effectivity of their naval blockade around the Philippines that no ship could have breached it. Hence, they now believe Esguerra's insistent and stubborn belief that these trucks of treasures are now in the Cordilleras. The only thing that Carlitos Leiza failed to know was the plan of the Americans on the said treasures.

Paul Roderick. A. Ysmael

The Final Chapter:
The Loss of the Trucks of Treasures

The Fall of Bessang Pass signaled the transfer of the theater of war from the romantic urban streets of Old Manila to the rugged but scenic trails of the Cordilleras. At that time Manila was known as the loveliest city of Asia while the Cordilleras was the most virgin among the pine forests in the world. In fact, despite the tailing dams of the various mines in the area that killed its major rivers, the Cordilleras is still the coolest and greenest part of the Philippines. After ravaging the womb of the modern city, the war now besmirched the pine forest's virginity. Blood of soldiers, young and old, within its creeks and ponds overflowed. The deer which was wild as the first summer wind was tamed by fear and even shed its

Paul Roderick. A. Ysmael

tears as it scampered to safety from the raining fire above. The fierce black boar, the king of this wilderness, shrieked and shouted as he avoided the thousands of bullets that darkened his path. The tough hornbill stopped pouncing on the old pine and stayed inside not only for a while but waited till the guns ceased their loud sounds of bang. The ethnic tribes that settled arguments with clan wars, ceased to be warriors and became witnesses of war at its ultimate viciousness. Here the heads are not cut, they are broken into pieces. The dead do not run into tens, it is now running in tens of hundreds. It is not about a family's honor or piece of land, it appears now that it is not even about country. It is not even about an eternal love, the kind that ignited the Trojan Wars. It is now simply about the trucks of treasures.

By the first week of July 1945, the Japanese Imperial forces assembled in the heartland of the Cordilleras, the best of what remains from their once indestructible war materiel and equipment in the Philippines. Their biggest guns which they used to guard their fortress in Bessang Pass are now gone together with their artillery crew but their mobile cannons, mortars and tanks are still roaring with fearless strides. They still have a force of about four thousand Japanese and Koreans and several thousands of Filipino Makapilis who acted as the Japanese constabulary force. Although with limited ammo, all of them are still armed, capable of killing an enemy and viciously dangerous. They still can withstand pocket skirmishes and can execute minor ambushes. After leaving their base in Bessang Pass, the Japanese forces spread themselves in the various

Paul Roderick. A. Ysmael

mountains in the Cordillera, splitting into small groups and then regrouping in order to stop their enemies' relentless pursuit. The Japanese set camp in the towns of Bakun in the west, Buguias in middle part of the Cordilleras and Bauko in the Mountain Provinces. They were also seen in Atok, Benguet and in Sagada, Mountain Province. Their main motivation is the possibility of escaping via the eastern Philippine coast or to hide in the mountains forever.

On the side of the Allied forces, the Americans viewed that the war in the Cordilleras is their last major battle before the end of World War II. So, all their land and air assets were now concentrated in the Cordilleras. They transformed the southern portion of the Tamaang Valley into an Airfield by laying temporary steel matting where two squadrons of small bombers and attack planes were stationed (until today, this portion of the Plains of Tamaang is still called the airfield). They pulled up into the mountains their newest Howitzers, some of them are still being used by the Philippine military. Their newly commissioned military jeeps, amphibious tanks and battle tanks rolled with victorious pride on the narrow trails beneath the green and majestic mountains. The various convoy of the still unscathed military equipment of the Allied forces look like the modern version of the chariots of the Ancient Roman centurions crossing the Rubicon. At a distance, where their engines cannot be heard, they seem to silently announce their victorious conquest of their enemy in a loud soundless presence. They are too huge for the narrow roads, too strong for their weary and tired adversaries and too modern to fight the five-years old

Paul Roderick. A. Ysmael

war. With the vibrant greenery as their landscape, the grey and green colored war materiel looked inappropriate but they forced their presence with ease as nothing can match their imposing strength. The Japanese only managed to fire and run, like what the Filipino guerillas did when Uncle Sam was miles away. They just shoot and run while waiting for the birth of the American twin beasts that finally annihilated the seat of Japan's military industry in the cities of Hiroshima and Nagasaki, courtesy of Enola Gay.

Nearly a month after the Fall of Bessang Pass, the protagonists of the war played the game of a cat and mouse in their wide playground called the Cordillera mountain ranges. Each time that the Americans find a Japanese camp, they capture it while the Japanese ran away and abandon it. They will soon find another hiding place until the American and Filipino forces would again discover it. Once again, they shall fire back and run again. There are too many hills and the forests are too thick in the Cordilleras that the game lasted for several months, weeks and days.

The game of hide and seek is too tiring for the one being sought and too frustrating for the one searching. The vastness of the Cordillera wilderness was too expansive for their game. Both armies are now too tired and frustrated that they now both wanted to end their battles. Although they are no longer directly engaging each other as the Japanese can no longer match up with the Allied forces, there were still unnecessary casualties from each other. Lives were still lost.

Paul Roderick. A. Ysmael

Yamashita's Trucks of Treasures

This was the environment where Col. Homa operated. They were being pursued by a small group of Filipinos determined to get the treasures and another group led by the Americans which is far more superior than his troops. So he decided to stop the game of hiding and went ahead to finish his mission. He decided to evade the Americans and face the weaker force of the Filipinos in one final battle, then proceed to Isabela and meet the Japanese submarines there. He sent scouts to locate Esguerra. Then, he issued orders to keep the Americans at bay and as far as possible from them so that the Filipinos cannot be aided by the Americans. He wanted to face his pursuers and let the trucks of treasures ran away from the Cordilleras towards the eastern Philippine seaboard. So, while he stayed put in Bauko town, the three trucks were already several kilometers away, travelling only by night and hiding during the day.

In the side of Esguerra, they had already reached the suburbs of the town of Bauko but decided to stay put and just follow the trucks until they can find a way of recovering the treasures. His men are already too tired to conduct an operation immediately. They know that the only way to get the treasures is to isolate them from Moha's main command by cutting into the convoy and then pulling away and ahead. They will then take the Cagayan Valley Road and proceed towards Ilocos Norte and surrender the treasures to the provincial authorities there and escort them towards Manila. As he has always emphasized to his men, the treasures are not for their personal gain. The country needs it to rebuild itself from the ravages of war. His plan which his commanders shared is just

Paul Roderick. A. Ysmael

take the treasures from the enemy and turn them over to Philippine authorities. Of course, he cannot prevent his men from taking a small piece of jewelry or some coins as the inventory may no longer be accurate but if he can give to the Government the bulk of the One trillion dollars' worth of treasures, the Philippines can have a hefty boost to be propelled as an economic power in Asia. At his age, he can still resume his practice of law which was derailed by the conquest of Manila and the departure of his law firm's clients. "Major Esguerra" obtained his law degree in 1939 from the UP College of Law. He immediately started practicing his profession and during the outbreak of the war, he had both American and German corporations as clients as well as most of the prominent Filipino and Spanish families. He gained prominence in the legal profession by defending himself while in jail when he was accused of murdering the political nemesis of his father. Aside from that, he topped the bar examinations. So he was really destined to be one of the country's most sought after legal counsel. Just like most of the guerilla officers who joined the force after the victory of the Japanese invaders, Esguerra did not plan to have a long military career. He just joined the guerilla forces to help in the fight for liberation. He was confident that after the war, he can return to his lucrative civilian life as a practicing lawyer. Hence, he knows that the recovery of the treasures is a higher patriotic purpose and not just an ordinary treasure hunt. Esguerra however did not know that as they were planning and taking their time, the treasures were slowly travelling farther and away from their eager hands. The trucks of

Paul Roderick. A. Ysmael

treasures slowly drifted away towards the east coast of the Philippines.

    The American cavalry contingent at that time already learned its lessons the hard way after the capture of Saulsberry. They stuck to the orders of their headquarters to just look for the trucks and report its location. They intently studied the terrain. They studied the behavior of their enemy. They learned how to observe and wait. They learned that patience is a virtue even during times of ultimate violence. For the first time in their military life, they applied everything they learned from their veteran instructors way back home who were part of the US Army during the Philippine-American war. Saulsberry now realized how unstable is the countries' relationships among each other. Just around forty years ago, as narrated by their instructors at West Point, the US Cavalry was shooting Filipino guerillas. He even read about the burning of Philippine villages by the American cavalry and also the absurd act of stealing a Catholic Church's bell to make it as a souvenir for winning a battle in small town somewhere in the Visayas. He and his classmates also heard about the bravery of the Muslim Filipinos in the south, who attacked soldiers ignoring the hail of bullets from the rifles of American infantrymen. This is the reason why the caliber 45 pistol was invented. In order to equip the Americans with a pistol that is powerful enough to put down a man or even a horse with one shot. One of his lecturers devoted three hours narrating his experience in the Southern Philippines about the warriors who cannot be intimidated by a pointed rifle simply because they are not afraid to die. They rather face

Paul Roderick. A. Ysmael

death than being subjects to American rule. The Filipino Muslim warriors were known to be attacking soldiers with mere bolos even if they sustained gunshots. In various occasions, the shot and wounded bolo-wielding "Moros" even inflicted fatal wounds against the American soldiers before expiring. They soon realized that these warriors were not only protecting their freedom, they were fighting for their Faith. With these thoughts about the Philippine battlefield and their recent experience, Saulsberry and his men were able to put their brains above their temper. They overcome the fear brought about by their first close encounter with their enemy. They learned fast. They now evaded any possible encounter and operated behind the bushes. They made themselves scarce and invisible and just reported the movements of the Japanese. Just when they were about to report that the trucks of treasure are in the town of Bauko, Mountain province, the Filipino guide overheard the locals talking about trucks that were sent ahead by the Japanese. Their invisible convoy is now a town away and several kilometers ahead. Saulsberry, through radio, reported their discovery to the US High Command in Baguio City.

Just a kilometer inside the Province of Ifugao, Moha's forces waited for Esguerra's men. They knew that some officers of the guerilla forces were using horses as means of travel. His Makapili scout said that they are travelling off-road and using short cuts. So, the Japanese commander scattered his men at the mouth of the Ifugao Province and was determined to slow down the pursuers of the treasures. This is now their 30th month inside the Cordillera heartland.

Paul Roderick. A. Ysmael

General Yamashita's forces are travelling in the opposite direction going to the caves of Sagada, Mountain Province. According to plan Yamashita will continue to be a decoy and look like the main Japanese force. The Japanese were confident that the only group interested on the treasures is a small guerilla band that happened to have discovered that the tale of the treasures is true and real. The disbelief of the Americans to the Esguerra's claim about the existence of the treasures was of no doubt, a great help to the Japanese plan to secretly send them to Japan. Until these last days of the war, the Japanese did not know that the Americans already knew and are also pursuing the treasures. This is the reason why they did not mind the escape of Saulsberry from the hands of their advance reconnaissance force in Bauko three days before. They considered Saulsberry's force as a cavalry company which lost its direction and incidentally saw them. In fact the reason why Moha hurriedly sent the trucks away is the possibility that the American cavalry will call for reinforcements and discover his main forces. They might "accidentally" discover the treasures. So instead of pursuing Saulsberry, his instincts dictated that it would be best to leave the town as early and as fast as possible before a large American contingent will discover them. So, here, just inside the Ifugao Province around 25 kilometers away from the famed Rice Terraces, he decided to took his stand against his immediate pursuers, the "E" Company of an unrecognized Filipino guerilla forces.

Being the reconnaissance group, Carlitos Leiza's group was always the first to meet Moha's men. With his commandeered military jeep, Carlitos and his men were advancing near the Mountain Province-Ifugao border at around ten in the morning on July 15, 1945. He aimed his binoculars around a hundred meters ahead of the dirt road when he noticed an unusual thing at the middle of the road. Fearing that it may be a hurriedly planted mine, he ordered his driver to halt. He sent a boloman to crawl near the digging and verify what devil it maybe. They were unaware at that time that a platoon of five Makapilis and two Korean conscripts were watching them. The platoon knew that their presence will soon be discovered. So, they established their firing positions. The boloman only manage to crawl for around two meters when machine gun fire from a huge Korean soldier rained on him. Impelled by sheer fear and adrenalin, the boloman hurled himself ten feet above the road from his crawling position and immediately docked behind a rock. The machine gun firing was so intense that the huge rock turned into a hundred thousand pebbles in just a matter of three minutes, but the boloman dug himself into the available space below the firing line. As the machine gun ceased firing and the dust cleared, Carlito's men and their jeep disappeared by fleeing towards the direction of their origin and in a curve, they hid their vehicle, covered it with bushes, got their rifles and went back to rescue their comrade. They climbed the right side of the mountain, above the road and higher than the position of their ambushers. Fast and silent, they gained vantage point. Carlito's used one shot to take out the machine gun wielding Korean and his six-foot frame was no match to the bullet that dug into his brain. They then fired at the Makapilis who sensing their disadvantaged position tried to run

Paul Roderick. A. Ysmael

away from the rushing bullets of the Filipino marksmen. Two Makapilis fell and the four others just ran away even leaving their rifles and fallen comrades. Angered by his near-death, the boloman rushed to the wounded Makapilis and used his full strength in chopping of their heads. Carlitos failed to restrain his man. He just ordered him to return to their camp in Cervantes. The boloman, Juan Cawag, would soon become an alcoholic and lived in the streets of Cervantes after the war.

With orders to engage, the Japanese contingent of around fifty men rushed towards the area of shooting. By that time, a company of Esguerra's men were already in the area in response to Carlitos' call for help. Fierce fighting was ignited when the Japanese fired their mortar hitting a bolomen formation and instantly killing three. Esguerra sent an advance force towards the front of the convoy to catch up the trucks of treasures. However, Moha was able to scarcely distribute his three hundred men in an area of around ten kilometers that the guerillas were forced to engage the Japanese first before finding the treasures. The Japanese occupied a long and narrow stretch inside Ifugao which forced Esguerra to also distribute his attacking men on the same stretch. The forces had no apparent advantage against each other. The Japanese force of around three hundred to four hundred men is just around of same capability to the Filipino force of around two hundred fifty to three hundred men. Being distributed in a mountainous stretch, some Filipino platoons were at higher point and some are at a disadvantaged point. The tanks cannot maneuver in the narrow trail with very steep slopes so they were

Paul Roderick. A. Ysmael

just operating as mounted guns and machineguns. Both forces have limited ammunition and food. They even lacked water. The battle was unplanned and by chance. It was fair game, with no superior advantage from other side. They were shooting at each other with no definite goals. It was a relentless shooting war for two days with no one wanting to sleep.

By July 17, 1945, the second day of their battle, Esguerra's composure crumbled. He did not plan to engage the Japanese in a long drawn battle. He did not plan to risk the lives of all his men just to fight a long war with the Japanese. Their mission is to swoop into enemy convoy and get the treasures. He cannot blame Carlitos as it was really a possibility as a reconnaissance patrol to engage the enemy once in a while in short skirmishes. Carlito's men were really intended for a cat and mouse game. It was necessary to track the enemy. He realized that the Japanese really planned this strategy to keep the treasures away from them. Esguerra also knew that these Japanese, being samurai warriors are ready to sacrifice their lives just to let the treasures reach Japan. He then decided to directly pursue the treasures wherever it may be located now. Esguerra selected a platoon of his most skilled men; they mounted themselves on their horses; moved away from the battlefield, and rode directly towards Northern Ifugao. He believed that the treasures are already near the town of Lagawe by this time. So he ordered his men to move at the fastest speed that they can ask from their steeds.

The horses from Abra are really dependable on rugged terrain, tall, with big agile bodies, sturdy legs

Paul Roderick. A. Ysmael

and great balancing capability they, can traverse mountains even without a trail. They gallop with authority and had the speed suitable for a pursuit of this nature.

As Esguerra's and Moha's forces were fighting it out in the Ifugao-Mountain Province border, the Americans were also preparing their move on the trucks of treasures. They have assembled their whole cavalry at Saddle Point to run after Moha. Two squadrons of bombers and attack planes from the Cervantes Airfield and Loakan Airport were also being readied. Before Leiza met Saulsberry, these developments were unknown to the battling groups in the area. It was their mutual impression that they are the only ones who were interested in the trucks of treasures. So, the Americans had all the undisturbed time preparing for their own pursuit.

With their reliable horses and intelligence support, Esguerra were able to pass by the stretch of Japanese positions travelling off-road along dangerous rocky cliffs and in between slippery mountain springs. It was a journey where men totally relied on the skill of their horses. The horses were so amazing that they can cross waterfalls, balance themselves on narrow trails and hop from one rock to another. They were in full speed and were very precise in their moves.

Before sunset, Esguerra and his men were about to hit the main road. They estimated that the trucks may be less than a kilometer ahead. Esguerra was about to give his attack instructions when suddenly, low-flying huge bomber planes suddenly roared above them surprising their horses who

Paul Roderick. A. Ysmael

responded with loud whines. The skies darkened as if the sunset immediately turned into late dusk due to the size and number of planes. As if sensing trouble, the proud steeds immediately halted against their masters' will. Before Esguerra can whip his horse to force obedience, he saw bombs raining like huge earthen jars from the sky about three hundred meters ahead. The twilight of dusk turned into a sharp light of sunrise in a matter of seconds and then with deafening loud blasts, the area became even brighter than a noontime sun of summer. The lights blinded the men and the horses. They only moved through their blind instincts. While they cannot see what is happening due to the extreme brightness that no human eye can bear, Esguerra knew that the Americans were blasting the mountains to bury whatever is ahead of them. The extent of the effect of these bombings was felt through tremors that affected as far as Bontoc in the West, Buguias in the South, Apayao in the North and Banaue, Ifugao in the East causing cracks on the world renowned Rice Terraces. In less than thirty minutes, five mountain peaks were flattened, the whole stretch of around five to eight kilometers of the trail was buried by landslides. Esguerra never saw exactly what were being buried by the Americans into oblivion but he was sure, these were the trucks of treasures!

Tomo, who was sitting beside the driver of the first truck of treasure seemed to have felt that time froze for a second. He heard nothing, he just saw an elongated steel dropping from the sky, followed by a strong light. He then felt himself flying with the trucks' debris and with several pieces of jewelry. He did not

Paul Roderick. A. Ysmael

feel any pain, he did not see any drop of blood. He just let himself be drowned by the light and enjoyed his peaceful flight upwards. He was in such a state when he realized that he was alone. He was flying with the tin box of treasures and the Great Golden Komodo. Tomo thanked his God for giving him the life that flashed back before him in two seconds. He thanked Him for fulfilling his dream to become a soldier and serve his Emperor. He thanked Him of making him a soldier worthy of the trust of his masters on earth. He thanked Him for allowing him to guard the treasures and dying for his country. Then he saw his father and mother welcoming him in a bright blissful place that looks like the peak of Mt. Fuji, a more serene and happy place. He smiled and realized that he has found peace, the greatest treasure on earth. On that fateful day, all the seventy-five Japanese soldiers, the three trucks of treasures and their escorting war vehicles and equipment were buried by avalanching rocks, earth, mud and pine trees. It was claimed by local folks that the trucks were blasted first, the impact tossed them into the deep ravines before the landslides engulfed them to be erased from the face of the earth and from the pages of history. They were buried too deep for metal detectors to locate; to be hidden both from the memory of those who may be able to remember and from the access of anyone who pursued them; and to be just a legend even to those who believed them as real.

The Japanese may have failed to bring the trucks of treasures to Japan, but they were successful enough to hide it in a place where no one can ever find them. In fact, it will soon be a word, that leaving the

Paul Roderick. A. Ysmael

trucks of treasures in the mountains was a deliberate alternative of the Japanese, and it seemed that the plan worked and was able to serve its purpose.

Amidst trembling grounds, cracking trails and falling rocks, Esguerra and his men were lucky enough to have the finest horses on earth. The stallions of Abra maneuvered in a perfectly synchronized fashion, avoiding the falling ground, stepping into the safest rocks and flying high from cliff to cliff like flying unicorns. They were smart enough to save their masters' lives. Despite their lack of vision, the animals' instincts made the men and horses reach a safer ground, two kilometers from where they started their retreat. For the first time in his life, Esguerra cursed the Americans, calling them the phantoms that destroyed his dreams for his country. He looked up at the returning planes and shouted at them invectives. A pilot, as if hearing what he was saying, pointed a dirty finger at him. He did not know that this is not the last time that the Americans will forsake him.

When all the planes left and after he saw the wreckage of the place, Esguerra was stunned in disbelief. All that he has worked in the war were vanished by the bomb. The ten kilometer stretch was too wide for a search. He gathered his men. He said that in a few hours, he is certain that American forces will cordon the area and he does not intend to fight them. They have no capability to fight them and they are not the enemy. He said that they have to leave immediately to evade the Americans. He thanked those who are still living and praised the memory of those who perished helping him hunting the trucks of

Paul Roderick. A. Ysmael

treasures. He ordered all his men to stop fighting Moha, return to their loved ones and start building their own treasures of family, livelihood and good health. He wished everyone good luck. He promised to just return and look for the trucks of treasures when the war was over. He bade good-bye to his friends. He ordered Miguel Moreno and Carlitos Leiza to return to the fold of the Philippine Army. He ordered Fungway and Benita Langbay to return to the Intelligence Service. He thanked Cirilo Ysmael for all his support and supplies that he managed to give to his men. He praised Anacleto Octaviano's brilliant utilization of his God-given size. Hiding his tears, he expressed his sincere gratitude for having these local heroes whose efforts may not even be included in our history of as a nation but their gallantry and dedication will always be the real treasures that he discovered during the war. With what remained of his men, Esguerra galloped westward, unmindful of whatever remains of the Japanese forces or whatever will be his fate in the Philippine military.

Just as Esguerra's forces left the place, the full US Cavalry Battalion arrived. They secured the area and were ordered to drive away any force that will try to recover the treasures. The American Government has decided to keep the treasures away from anyone. It was later on explained to Esguerra that the Americans and their allies decided to hide the treasures not only from the warring countries but also in the history of the war. The allies were of the belief that if the treasures are found, all countries beginning from Iraq to Malaysia would lay claim to it. It may again trigger another dispute and may not lead the

Paul Roderick. A. Ysmael

peaceful conclusion of World War II. The treasures are owned by ancient Asian kingdoms that has descendants from West Asia to the Far East. It may be claimed by states, kingdoms, sultanates, fiefdoms and even by small bands of conquest from and by ancient generations to another, it would be best that they shall be buried along with the violent and inhuman memories of the war. It was a decision very difficult to make, but for those leaders who really felt the pains of war and witnessed the tragic and wasteful loss of human lives, the attainment of peace was the most valuable treasure that they preferred.

What made matters more complex, was the fact that no one ever recorded the exact place where the bombings to hide the treasures took place. All the treasure hunters today can only say that the bombing of the trucks of treasures happened "somewhere in the heart of the Cordilleras." With mountains that look exactly like each other, with ravines and cliffs that are all ruggedly identical and with frequent landslides and perpetually changing topography, the trucks of treasures continued to be undiscovered until today. From one man's dream, it became a legend, it is now myth and perhaps, it may soon be erased from human memory.

Perhaps, we were not able to pay the price that the trucks of treasures demanded. With its legendary value, it may be worth more than a thousand lives, but our leaders then were so careful not to waste so many lives of men for such treasures. Esguerra always told us that he wants everyone in the group to taste the economic benefits that our country may have if we

Paul Roderick. A. Ysmael

were able to recover those treasures. He did not want us to die fighting for it. Such desire may have lessened the price that we were offering to get it. I believe that each treasure has its corresponding price. You can never get something of value without paying for it. Look at our river, because of our desire to have gold, we deprived your generation and the generations next, the once emerald green and blue water that even salmons used to populate. The mines killed the river and made its waters brown and sometimes red. For the gold that we cannot even see, we paid it with hundreds of livestock that were killed, with rice fields that can no longer be tilled and with the river that no longer lives," Cirilo Ysmael, my late grandfather remarked, as he looked at the dead Abra River, the victim of the mining operations of Lepanto Mines. Shaking his head, he then finished his tale about the trucks of treasure with a sad grin, "Just like the trucks of treasures that were not enough to buy peace, the gold that comes from the mines cannot pay for the Abra River that once flowed, with a clean living water amidst the heart of the Gran Cordillera, which gave us real life. Sometimes we treasure things that are precious not because they matter, but only because they glitter.

Paul Roderick. A. Ysmael

Postscript

Paul Roderick. A. Ysmael

No one can tell for sure if the convoy that the Americans bombed into oblivion and buried under the avalanche of five mountain tops was carrying Yamashita's trucks of treasures. As Esguerra's men claimed, they were kilometers away from the convoy when the bombing took place. If you are familiar with the Cordillera road system and terrain, it was really impossible for them to see if the trucks were really there. There was also no reported survivor from the Japanese convoy who could have told if indeed the trucks were still with them when the Americans decided to erase them from the trails and even erasing the trail itself. There are claims that Yamashita did not really send the trucks of gold to Moha. From the start, the trucks with Moha are already diversionary trucks. Some claim that Yamashita buried the trucks within the vicinity of Bessang Pass because at that time he already knew that he cannot escape any longer and that he was just waiting his capture. Some had accounts seeing trucks being buried near the Mankayan-Cervantes Boundary. Some claim it to have been buried near the Banaue Rice Terraces. Lastly, there was an account that the trucks were buried near a military camp in Baguio City. Some folks claim that it was necessary for the Government forces to neutralize Albert Fungway because he knew the location of the treasures and he had a misunderstanding with the officer with respect to the "sharing" for the said treasure. All these claims were not verified and remain unproven. But amidst these claims, there are two things that remain uncontroverted (1) Yamashita's Trucks of Treasures really existed and (2) where ever were Yamashita's trucks were hidden or buried, are not yet discovered.

Paul Roderick. A. Ysmael

It appears however that those who took part in the pursuit for the treasures were able to find their own gold and jewels from the rich bosom of the Cordilleras:

Anacleto Octaviano, inherited a sugarcane farm and several hectares of rice land from his Angkay Elmo. He operated small sugar mills and factories using old and manual techniques to produce sugar. He was the number one producer of organic muscovado sugar in Cervantes and sold rice to the mountain towns of the Cordilleras. He also made the best of the town's traditional rice pillow called *sinambong* and the *balicucha*, a native sugar candy, both are still produced in Cervantes until this date. He died of diabetes sometime in the early 1990s. His grandchildren and great grandchildren remain to be the best farmers in town.

Albert Fungway became the regional head of the national intelligence group of the military during the time of President Ramon Magsaysay and was responsible in the defeat of the communist insurgency in Northern Luzon. He retired in Bontoc and became a tribal adviser and community organizer. He made a living exporting Civet Cat Coffee to the United States while helping the late Macliing Dulag in his fight against the construction of the Chico River Dam to save their ancestral lands from being flooded. He was "accidentally killed" by the Philippine Constabulary during their encounter with the New People's Army near the Chico River Delta in 1979 where he was training villagers on organic farming.

Paul Roderick. A. Ysmael

Benita Langbay, retired as a major in the Philippine Army Medical Corps. She never married but in 1974, Toki visited her and took her to Japan. According to her relatives, she is still alive and communicating to them via her Facebook account. She is still pretty at 89 years old. She recently added me as a facebook friend.

Carlitos Leiza, returned to the Philippine Army, his last post was an assignment with the Philippine Expeditionary Forces to Korea (PEFTOK) during the Korean War where he commanded a platoon of Philippine Scouts that infiltrated North Korea to steal the war map detailing a chemical weapons attack on UN forces. This prevented the use of WMD chemicals against UN Forces near the 38th parallel. He never returned to Cervantes until today.

Cirilo Ysmael, returned to farming and rice milling. He continued writing scripts and directing the "Comedia" every annual town fiesta until Martial Law was proclaimed and the national curfew prohibited staging of late night shows. His store is still serving his neighbors until this time but his rice mill has long been gone.

Angel Moreno, did not return to military service, instead, he developed their hacienda and tried exporting citrus and coffee to Spain and Mexico.

Marcial Esguerra, became President of the Philippines until removed by the Americans following a popular uprising in 1986. To discredit both himself and the legend of the trucks of treasures, several historians and military experts aired doubts on his

Paul Roderick. A. Ysmael

military exploits and questioned his medals. But for those who lived and fought with him, they will always attest that he deserved every medal attached to his suit. He was the best fighting guerilla officer of World War II. It was believed that the small black plane that were flying low between the tall mountains in the Cordilleras during Martial Law years were sent by him to detect the locations of the Trucks of Treasures.

Fabian Ver, had a brilliant military career. Closely associated with Esguerra, he rose to become the highest ranking military officer of the Philippines.

Col. Makoto Moha, was never heard after the Battle of Bauko. He is believed to be one of those Japanese stragglers who settled in Barangay Bao-angan, in the southern part of Cervantes, near Benguet where a community of Japanese-looking "natives" have settled, inter-marrying with the locals. He is suspected of having propagated the "giant Bao-angan Chicken" the largest chicken in the country today.

Toki Yamamoto, was able to escape to Japan where he had a successful business exporting Kobe beef or wagyu to the United States. After the death of his first wife, he looked for Benita Langbay in the Philippines. He took Benita to Japan in 1974. He still shows the receiving slip of the treasure maps that he gave to the Japanese officer in the Imperial Palace, in case somebody asks for them. He always denies that his group recovered some gold bars in Bessang Pass in 1974 and insistent in his claim that their visit to Bessang Pass was for sentimental purpose. Rumors persist, however that they recovered a box containing

Paul Roderick. A. Ysmael

24 gold bars and gave half of it to the President of the Philippines.

Cervantes, Ilocos Sur, was recently proclaimed the "Summer Capital of Ilocos Region" because of its pine forests that resembles that of Baguio City in Benguet and its majestic waterfalls that both

Paul Roderick. A. Ysmael

contribute to the cool climate in its western mountainous villages. Contributing to this accolade is the historic Bessang Pass and the grandeur of its height and victorious past. However, the largest river that flows at its eastern side, the Abra River is still suffering allegedly from the past mining operations of a nearby mine and now from the hands of small pocket miners. Brown water still runs through it and the water is still not safe for both agricultural purpose or human consumption.

And this rural legend of the trucks of treasures still persists. I hope someday we will learn to treasure the lessons from these treasures, which I believe are more valuable than those tons of gold and diamonds that were lost.

Paul Roderick. A. Ysmael

Kaibigan Books Publisher

Kaibigan Books, Los Angeles, California, U.S.A.
Percival Campoamor Cruz
percivalcruz@yahoo.com

Published Books -
"May Bagwis ang Pag-ibig"
Percival Campoamor Cruz
Jobo Elizes (Publisher)
"The Maiden of Ilog-Pasig"
Percival Campoamor Cruz
"Si Kumareng Cougar"
Percival Campoamor Cruz
"Mga Tilamsik ng Isip"
Augusto de Leon

Paul Roderick. A. Ysmael

Yamashita's Trucks of Treasures

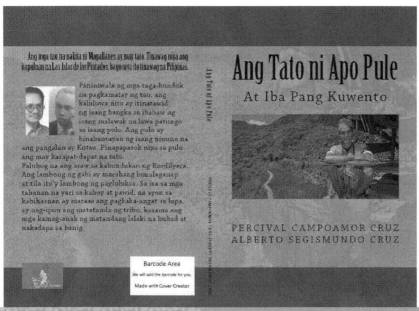

Paul Roderick. A. Ysmael

Paul Roderick. A. Ysmael

Paul Roderick. A. Ysmael

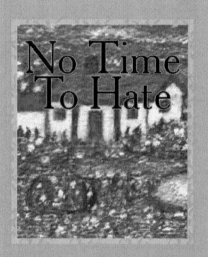

"Ang Tato ni Apo Pule"
Percival Campoamor Cruz
"Sariling Parnassus"
Alberto Segismundo Cruz
"Drama Queen"
Percival Campoamor Cruz
"Ang Kapangyarihan ng Kanyang Pag-ibig"
Percival Campoamor Cruz
"No Time to Hate"
Milton Goodwin
"The Human in Man"

Paul Roderick. A. Ysmael

Dr. Feodor F. Cruz, Ph.D
"Taxation in the Philippines"
Tomas P. Matic, Jr., Llb.
"Flavors of the Philippines"
Anita Sese-Schon

Paul Roderick. A. Ysmael

Paul Roderick. A. Ysmael

Coming Soon Book Projects

"Why I Am a Spiritist"
E. Filamor

"Iris – Ang Reyna ng Sandaigdig na Kulay"
Alberto Segismundo Cruz

"Tatlong Nobelang Filipino"
Alberto Segismundo Cruz

"Tatlong Larawan ng Pag-ibig"
Vic Macapagal

Paul Roderick. A. Ysmael

Yamashita's Trucks of Treasures

Paul Roderick. A. Ysmael

Made in the USA
Monee, IL
09 February 2020